Editor's Foreword

By James Whitaker, Royal Columnist for the Daily Mirror.

Fifty years have passed since a somewhat shy, hesitant Princess Elizabeth succeeded to her throne as Queen Elizabeth II, following the death of her father at the tragically young age of 56. Her Majesty had neither wished, nor expected this. She was just 25 and the mother of two small children. But, instantly accepting the duties of this onerous office, she has, ever since, steered an unerring course.

Unceasingly, her considerable will and intellect have been directed towards serving her country and those countries that make up her great Commonwealth. There are few, even the most obdurate of republicans, who could fail to concede that her tireless duty and devotion have ensured resounding success in this demanding role. At times it has been no easy task. The Eighties, and particularly the Nineties, witnessed events involving members of her family and those close to them, that left her weary and upset.

This year has also brought great tragedy to the Queen with the deaths of both her sister, Princess Margaret, Countess of Snowdon and Queen Elizabeth, the Queen Mother within a few weeks of one another. Yet she has been able to draw great strength from the love and loyalty of her family and the people. True monarch that she is, the Queen has never allowed anything, even profound personal misfortune, to prevent her from fulfilling her duty. Her two guiding lights throughout have been the example and wisdom of King George VI, and a strong belief in God. Her Majesty doted on her father and has followed all the sage advice he gave her while, throughout her life, she has remained a devout, practicing Christian.

At the time of her Coronation in June 1953 she vowed to reign until death. In the spectacular ceremony at Westminster Abbey she was anointed with holy oil. The simple fact that she took an oath before God ensures there will be no abdication. The idea has never crossed her mind, let alone that of anybody else within her court.

Her Majesty still enjoys, more than anything, the simple pleasures - lengthy walks with her many dogs and even longer horse rides while at Windsor, Sandringham or her beloved Balmoral Castle in Scotland. It's a pity that few have had the opportunity to see the 'unofficial' Queen. She has a dry sense of humour, a naughty, but never unkind, side to her nature while she is famous for being an excellent mimic, particularly of those who act pompously.

As much, if not more, than any of us, Her Majesty has been looking forward to the celebrations and carefully planned visits throughout the country from May to August. I am sure we all wish her well in this her Golden Jubilee year.

Her Majesty Queen Elizabeth II

Head of the Commonwealth

MESSAGE FROM
HER MAJESTY QUEEN ELIZABETH II

Prince Philip and I have been deeply touched by the many kind messages about the Golden Jubilee.

This anniversary is for us an occasion to acknowledge with gratitude the loyalty and support which we have received from so many people since I came to the Throne in 1952. It is especially an opportunity to thank all those of you who help others in your own local communities through public or voluntary service. I would like to think that your work will be particularly recognised during this Jubilee year.

I hope also that this time of celebration in the United Kingdom and across the Commonwealth will not simply be an occasion to be nostalgic about the past. I believe that, young or old, we have as much to look forward to with confidence and hope as we have to look back on with pride.

I send my warmest good wishes to you all.

ELIZABETH R.

6th February, 2002.

The Right Hon. Tony Blair, MP

Prime Minister

10 DOWNING STREET
LONDON SW1A 2AA

MESSAGE FROM THE PRIME MINISTER

I am pleased to be able to announce that Her Majesty The Queen has approved a number of recommendations for the programme of celebrations during 2002, the focal point of which will be the 'Jubilee weekend' period covering 1 to 4 June. As I announced on 23 November 2000, Tuesday 4 June will be a Bank Holiday in place of the Spring Bank Holiday that would otherwise fall on 27 May 2002, and Monday 3 June will be an additional Bank Holiday for the Golden Jubilee.

Following the recent re-organisation of government departments, the Ministerial Committee set up last year to help co-ordinate arrangements with Buckingham Palace is now being chaired by the Secretary of State for Culture, Media and Sport.

This significant national anniversary of fifty years of The Queen's reign will offer people of all ages and cultures and from all walks of life the opportunity for celebration, and the events surrounding the Jubilee will provide numerous opportunities for voluntary and community service. It should be a time for looking forward as well as back - including at the great changes that have taken place in the nation's life during Her Majesty's reign.

Tony Blair

HER ROYAL HIGHNESS THE PRINCESS ROYAL

PRESIDENT

SAVE THE CHILDREN

Save the Children

Message from Save the Children

Save the Children is delighted to be the official charity to benefit from the publication 'Her Majesty & The Commonwealth: 50 Golden Years'.

The money raised from the sales of this book will be used to help support Save the Children's work in the UK and across the world. The Golden Jubilee provides an opportunity for millions of people to celebrate The Queen's reign and to honour her unstinting work and successes. There is also another significant celebration taking place this year – Her Majesty will have been patron of Save the Children for 50 years.

Back in 1952, it was noted that: "As Princess, Queen Elizabeth II's involvement included receiving officials of Save the Children and a party of children from the junior clubs at Buckingham Palace in 1948, and a little more than a year ago Her Majesty made an informal and conversational inspection of the Save the Children fund's team in Greece. The Save the Children Fund continues to be the only voluntary society in the Commonwealth, of which Her Majesty is head, which is concerned solely with the relief of children and the promotion of child welfare without regard to their race, nation, colour or creed. We derive high encouragement from her Majesty's gracious interest in our work."

Times have changed since 1952 but we are still delighted to have Her Majesty's Patronage and support.

Save the Children would like to thank those organisations and individual who have contributed to our work. In particular, we would like to thank Faircount Ltd, the publisher of 'Her Majesty & The Commonwealth – 50 Golden Years' for inviting Save the Children to benefit from the project.

Mike Aaronson

Mike Aaronson
Director General

Registered office:
The Save the Children Fund
17 Grove Lane
London SE5 8RD

Telephone 020 7703 5400
Fax 020 7703 2278
www.savethechildren.org.uk

"Save the Children organisations in UK, Australia, Canada and New Zealand will benefit from the sale of this book."

London Underground has a long and loyal history of supporting and participating in Royal events and can count the Queen as one of our customers when she opened the Victoria line in 1969.

Today the Tube carries three million customers a day and delivering Londoners and visitors safely to and from major events and celebrations is something in which we continue to take great pride.

We are the world's oldest metro and are as proud of our heritage as we are of the stunning new extension to the Jubilee line – whose stations have won many awards and the praise of both regular customers and travellers from home and abroad.

We have been working for many months with our partners at Transport *for* London and the rail companies to ensure the celebrations in London are fully supported by public transport services over the Golden Jubilee weekend. Those services will include, for only the third time in our history, a service throughout the day and night on 3-4 June.

As we congratulate Her Majesty and celebrate the past 50 years, we also look to the future. New trains, new track, new signals and new-look stations will ensure the Underground serves future generations and helps to keep London at the heart of the Commonwealth.

To find out more about London Underground, and about public transport services during the Golden Jubilee celebrations, visit our website at **www.thetube.com.**

THE QUEEN'S GOLDEN JUBILEE 2002

UNDERGROUND

www.thetube.com

Her Majesty and the Commonwealth

50 Golden Years

Contents

Then & Now

Public Life

Private Life

Writers' Biographies

Editor – James Whitaker

A well liked and charismatic commentator whose depth of knowledge, combined with his frank and forthright manner have made him one of the leading authorities on the modern monarchy. The reputation he has gained during his long tenure as the Daily Mirror's royal correspondent has made him one of the most sought after and high profile figures in royal media circles.

Robert Lacey

Ex-Sunday Times correspondent, Robert Lacey can justifiably claim to be THE biographer of the Queen. A British historian and writer who specialises in getting close to - and alongside - his subjects. His Silver Jubilee biography, "Majesty", was greeted with instant critical acclaim on both sides of the Atlantic, selling more than a million copies world-wide. It remains acknowledged as the definitive study of British monarchy - a subject on which Robert continues to write and lecture in Britain and other countries. Noted for his original research and for making vital social issues accessible to the general reader in a compulsive, page-turning style, Robert is the author of numerous bestsellers.

Dickie Arbiter

Formerly a press officer at Buckingham Palace, in charge of the Royal Collection PR. Still "helps out" at the Palace press office and is on secondment to assist with the huge workload the Golden Jubilee will undoubtedly create. Ex LBC broadcaster and now a commentator for the BBC and ITN.

Harold Brooks-Baker

Publisher of Burke's Peerage, the most famous reference work for the nobility. An American who dresses in an eccentrically English style, his knowledge of the aristocracy and protocol is unsurpassed. He makes regular appearances on British television, as well as CNN including the Larry King Live show.

Richard Kay

The Daily Mail's Royal correspondent for the past 14 years, he was a good friend and media adviser to Princess Diana. Much favoured by those who look after Prince Charles at St James's Palace, he receives very thorough briefings from them. Recently invited to Highgrove, Charles's Gloucestershire home, as HRH's guest.

Robert Hardman

Brilliant columnist and senior feature writer on the Daily Mail. Formerly Royal Reporter for The Daily Telegraph, Robert enjoys a large following amongst the influential movers and shakers and is surely destined to be an editor in the near future. Well regarded by Buckingham Palace on account of his interesting, and very accurate, stories.

Jennie Bond

The BBC's much loved royal reporter. Enthusiastically cheered when walking down the Mall or outside Buckingham Palace while reporting or preparing to do so. Well briefed by all the various royal factions.

Ron Allison

Former correspondent for the BBC, before making his name as Press Secretary to the Queen (1973-78). Now works for ITN as a senior Royal Court reporter. In very good favour at Buckingham Palace and frequently airs his views on royal matters. Co-wrote THE definitive book on the royals, "The Royal Encyclopaedia".

Gyles Brandreth

Former MP, brilliant broadcaster and writer on a wide range of subjects. He has recently been making his mark on matters royal, including an excellent recent interview with Prince Philip and with the Hon. Margaret Rhodes, who was at the bedside of the Queen Mother when she died. Consistently entertaining and seemingly able to gain access which is denied to all others.

Iwona Whitaker

Iwona Whitaker, wife of editor, James Whitaker, has written several cook books, including two on the likes and dislikes of the Royal Family. She regularly contributes recipes and articles to magazines and formerly ran her own catering company.

Golden Jubilee Project
100 Pall Mall
St. James's
London SW1Y 5HP
Tel: +44 (0)20 7664 8840
Fax: +44 (0)20 7664 8841
email: mail@er50.com

Design and production
The Conservatory / Apex Group, London NW3

Picture editing
Photographers Intenational

Photographic credits
Cover photograph by John Swannell, Camera Press

All other photographs supplied by:
Anwar Hussein
Camera Press
Corbis
Getty Images/Hulton
Press Association
Terry Le Goubin
The Royal Collection
©2002, Her Majesty Queen Elizabeth II (pages 194-203)
Photographers International

Project Marketing
Charles Anderson
Andrew Hanson
Peter Martin
Lloyd Millett
Robert Sinclair

Printed in UK
Save the Children will receive 25% of the cover price for each copy of this book that is sold. Revenues derived from commercial partnerships, including advertising and sponsorship in connection with this title, do not directly or indirectly benefit Save the Children. Save the Children is a registered charity, UK registration 1076822.

Pour chaque exemplaire vendu, Save the Children recevra 25% du prix de vente indiqué en couverture. Save the Children ne bénéficie ni directement ni indirectement des recettes provenant de partenariats commerciaux, y compris la publicité et les parrainages liés à ce livre. Save the Children est une œuvre de bienfaisance reconnue d'utilité publique, inscrite au Royaume-Uni sous le numéro 1076822.

Published by Faircount Ltd.
on behalf of the Golden Jubilee Project

ISBN 0-9531900-9-9

MARKS & SPENCER
LIZ TAYLOR
Counsellor
Cruse Bereavement Care
MARKS & SPENCER
TONY GINTY
Parent Governor
Nascot Wood Schools
MARKS & SPENCER
MICHAEL CATER
Superintendent
St John Ambulance
MARKS & SPENCER
KIM PERFETT
Fundraiser
Marie Curie Cancer Care
MARKS & SPENCER
SYLVIA UNWIN
Volunteer Visitor
Age Concern
MARKS & SPENCER
FREDA PINNER
Community Representative
Youth Offending Panel

Elizabeth II

Golden Jubilee Queen

By Robert Lacey

The baby born at 17 Bruton Street, Mayfair, on 21st April 1926 was not thought of as a future queen. When her parents, Prince Albert, Duke of York, and his wife, the former Elizabeth Bowes-Lyon, discussed their daughter's name with her grandfather, King George V, the Queen Victoria question came up.

Above
An angelic looking Princess Elizabeth, pictured in 1927 at the age of 1, at St Paul's Walden Bury in Hertfordshire, the home of her grandparents Lord and Lady Strathmore. Princess Elizabeth's parents, the then Duke and Duchess of York, went on an extended tour of Australia and New Zealand in 1927 and pictures were taken of their young daughter and sent out to them.

Right
The Queen poses in full regalia for a historic photograph taken by Cecil Beaton on her Coronation day in 1953.

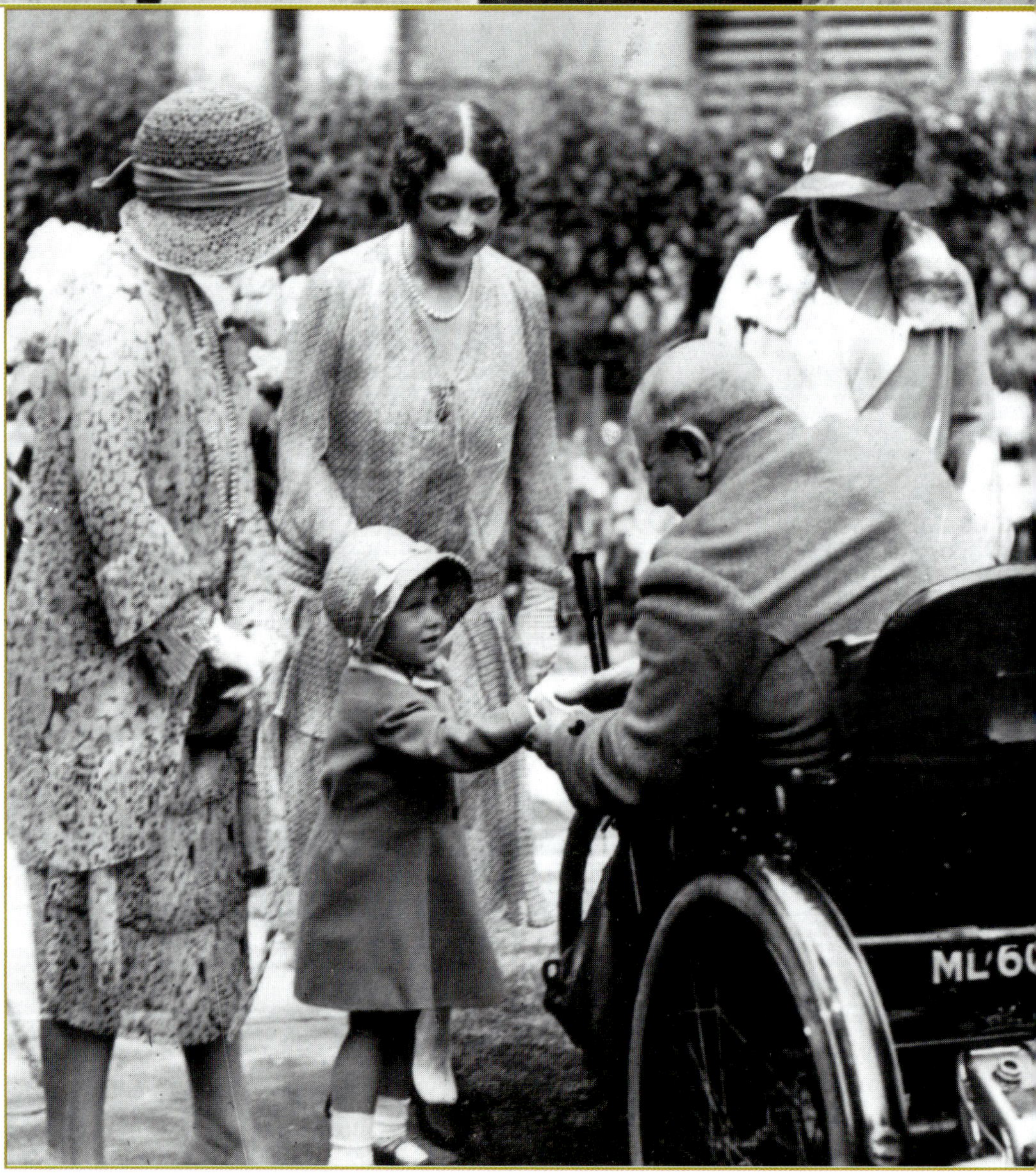

"We are so anxious for her first name to be Elizabeth," wrote her father, "as it is such a nice name." While the King agreed it was "a pretty name", it did worry him that his younger son had said "nothing about Victoria". The great Queen Empress had decreed that the names of all children close to the direct line of succession should perpetuate the memory of her beloved Albert or herself.

"I hardly think that necessary," George V decided on reflection. Princess Elizabeth was not in the direct line of succession to the throne, and the little girl would be pushed further down the list if her parents had a son.

Top
A group photograph taken at Buckingham Palace after the Christening. In the back row: the Duke of Connaught, King George V, the Duke of York and the Earl of Strathmore. In the front row: the Lady Elphinstone, Queen Mary, the Duchess of York (with Princess Elizabeth), the Countess of Strathmore and Princess Mary.

Bottom
Princess Elizabeth at about 3.

Princess Elizabeth on the platform at King's Cross station about to depart with her Royal grandparents for Christmas holidays at Sandringham.

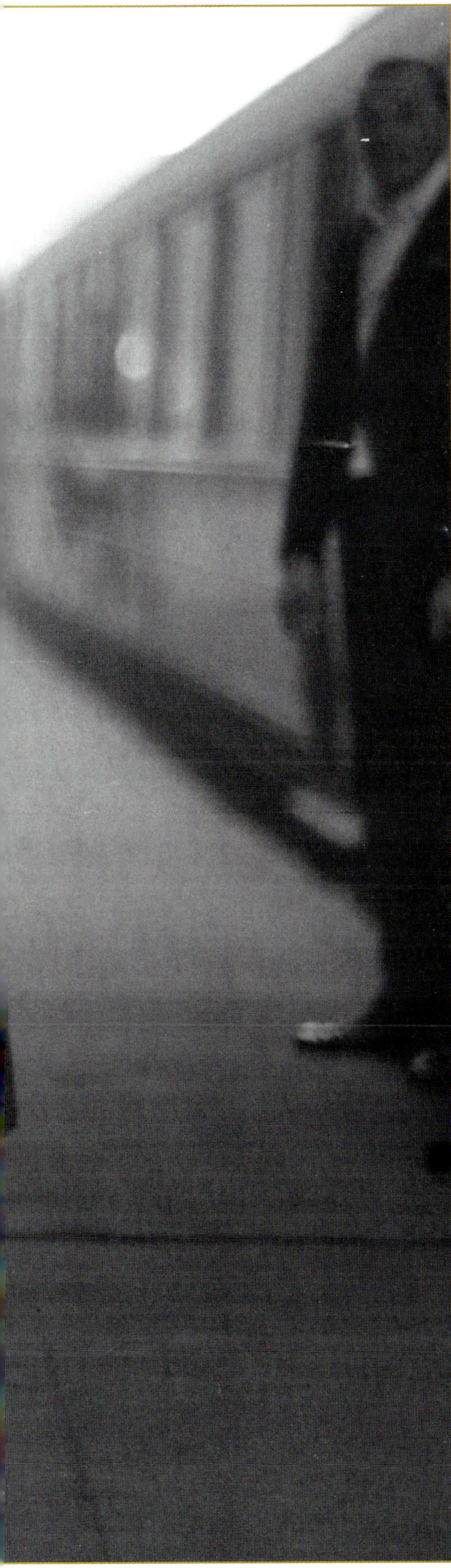

Spending her early years without the burden of being groomed for monarchy contributed greatly to the matter-of-fact and modest style that has marked the life and work of Elizabeth II. Her mother, who never went to school herself, felt that childhood should be fun, storing up "lots of pleasant memories," and she set about ensuring this for Elizabeth and her next child, who turned out to be a girl — the Princess Margaret Rose, born in August 1930. The two sisters' childhood education was entrusted to an energetic young Scottish governess, Marion Crawford, "Crawfie", whose story book tales of the "Little Princesses" would later become world-wide best-sellers. History, geography and bible-reading were mixed with singing, drawing, music and dancing — and also riding lessons. Horses were to become the great passion of Elizabeth II.

The abdication in December 1936 of Princess Elizabeth's quicksilver Uncle David, King Edward VIII, transformed her life. Lady Cynthia Asquith was visiting the little princesses on Abdication day and caught sight of an envelope on the hall table addressed to "the Queen".

"That's Mummie now, isn't it?" said the 10-year-old Princess Elizabeth gravely. When Crawfie explained to the little girls that they were going to live in Buckingham Palace, they looked at her in horror. "What!" said 'Lilibet'. "You mean forever?"

Top
In regal pose: Princess Elizabeth, aged nine months, photographed in January 1927. Beside her is a photograph of her mother. Her parents, the Duke and Duchess of York, were then on an extended tour of Australia and New Zealand and monthly photographs were taken between December 1926 and June 1927 and sent out to them.

Middle
The proud grandmother: Princess Elizabeth pictured in 1927 at the age of 1 in her pram, with her grandmother Lady Strathmore in the grounds of her home at St Paul's Walden Bury Hertfordshire. The young princess' parents, then Duke & Duchess of York, spent a lot of 1927 overseas on an extended tour of Australia and New Zealand.

Bottom
Tired: the Duchess of York tries to cajole Princess Elizabeth into posing for the camera – without success. This picture was taken in February 1931. [Credit: Marcus Adams]

An historic study of Her Majesty Queen Elizabeth II, then Princess Elizabeth, taken in November 1934, when she was 11 years old. She is seen in bridesmaid's outfit for the wedding of her uncle, the Duke of Kent, to Princess Marina.

Courtiers speculated that the new King George VI, just forty-one, and his wife, aged thirty-six, might now try for a son. But the King and Queen seemed to have looked at the serious and dutiful character of their elder daughter, and to have felt she was admirably suited to the job of constitutional monarch. Talking to the poet and essayist Osbert Sitwell one night in the 1930s, her father compared Princess Elizabeth to Queen Victoria - then gave Sitwell a very direct and meaningful look. "From the first moment of talking," said the future George VI, "she showed so much character, that it was impossible not to wonder whether history would not repeat itself." With her thirteenth birthday in April 1939, the princess started her formal training — constitutional history lessons with Sir Henry Marten, the vice-provost of Eton, a beloved and whimsical character, known for sucking on his handkerchief, comforter-like, as he paced around the chaos of his book-strewn study. Marten taught the princess the intricacies of Parliamentary democracy, the difference between adjourning, proroguing and dissolving Parliament and all the other technicalities over which she would one day preside. But for Elizabeth, the great event of that year — which also saw the outbreak of World War II — was her decisive encounter in July at Dartmouth Naval College with her lively, blond, Viking-like cousin, Prince Philip of Greece, then eighteen. The couple had met before. Philip was the nephew of "Uncle Dickie", Lord Louis Mountbatten, and had already made his mark in royal circles. "I like Philip," George VI would say a few years later. "[He] thinks about things in the right way."

Top left
Elizabeth Duchess of York at a railway station with her two daughters, Princess Elizabeth and Princess Margaret. Princess Elizabeth has one of the family's corgis on a leash.

Top right
Royal sisters: Princess Elizabeth, now Queen Elizabeth II, pictured in August 1932 at the age of 6, with her younger sister Princess Margaret.

Middle
The Princess at the zoo with Miss Crawford (Crawfie).

Bottom
Royal Thespians, December 1941. L to r, Queen Elizabeth, Princess Margaret and Princess Elizabeth during rehearsal of 'Cinderella', the first royal pantomime at Windsor Castle. The two princesses are in costume for their parts.

Royalty and Nanny, May 1939. Princess Elizabeth and her sister Princess Margaret with their Nanny Miss Marion Crawford leaving the headquarters of the YMCA in London.

There was an outbreak of mumps at the naval college and Philip, deputed to entertain the princesses, took the thirteen-year-old Elizabeth for a game of croquet. A snapshot of the time shows the handsome prince in his midshipman's uniform staring hard at the croquet hoops on the lawn. Facing him is the child-like figure of Princess Elizabeth staring hard at him.

The Queen later acknowledged that that was the moment when she fell "in love". War sent the cousins their separate ways, Philip to sea and Elizabeth to "somewhere in the country" — which was actually Windsor Castle, in a curious extension of her secluded childhood. While war gave most teenagers the excitement and license of being adults before their time, the two little princesses were packed up and stowed away for the duration, like Buckingham Palace's Sevres porcelain — national treasures.

The two constants for the princess were her constitutional lessons and her correspondence with Philip, whom she had decided, in her practical and single-minded manner, that she would marry. With the ending of war, she applied herself to this, persuading her reluctant parents to overcome the barriers created by Philip's Greek citizenship and by the feeling, shared by both the King and the Queen, that Elizabeth had scarcely met any eligible young men of her own age. Queen Elizabeth, the future Queen Mother, drew up a "First XI" of suitors for her elder daughter, and she did not select Philip to open the batting. Her preference was for young English aristocrats like "Porchie," the horse-mad Lord Porchester, the future Earl of Carnarvon. But while the princess enjoyed talking horses with Porchie — he would later become her racing manager — she had never had the slightest doubt that the unconventional, quirky-minded and thoroughly undeferential Philip was the man for her.

In the autumn of 1946, the twenty-five-year-old Philip proposed, the princess accepted, and her father consented to the match, provided it remained secret until after her twenty-first birthday, which would occur while the King, Queen and their two daughters were on a long-scheduled tour of South Africa.

Top left
Regal composure: Princess Elizabeth poses for the camera in March 1939, six months before the outbreak of World War II.

Middle left
Family gathering, 1942

Below left
1940

Middle
Princess Elizabeth driving a truck as part of the war effort

Top right
King George VI (1895 – 1952) with his wife Queen Elizabeth and their daughters Princess Elizabeth and Princess Margaret at Royal Lodge in Windsor, July 1946.

Below right
The 1947 tour of South Africa: despite the yearning for Lt. Philip Mountbatten RN, to whom she had recently become engaged, Princess Elizabeth and her sister Princess Margaret had great fun during their 1947 trip to Africa and are seen here (centre) during a swimming party at the Victoria Falls Hotel in Rhodesia (Zimbabwe).

Far right
Princess Elizabeth at Buckingham Palace in 1942

The princess made a memorable broadcast to mark her coming of age. "I declare before you all," she said, "that my whole life, whether it be long or short, shall be devoted to your service and the service of our great Imperial Commonwealth to which we all belong."

The engagement was announced on her return from South Africa and was greeted with delight by austerity-ridden Britain — "a flash of colour," as Winston Churchill described it, "on the hard road we have to travel." The couple were married on 20 November 1947. "I was so proud of you & thrilled at having you so close to me on our long walk in Westminster Abbey," her father wrote to her later. "But when I handed your hand to the archbishop, I felt that I had lost something very precious... I can see that you are sublimely happy with Philip, which is right, but don't forget us is the wish of Your ever-loving & devoted Papa."

The princess's early years of marriage were the closest she would ever come to living an "ordinary" life. As the wife of serving officer Lieutenant Philip Mountbatten RN, she followed her husband to Malta, shopped with real money in the island's winding streets, went to the hairdressers and had picnics on the beach. Her first two children, Charles and Anne, were born in 1948 and 1950, between tours of naval duty.

" I declare before you all, that my whole life, whether it be long or short, shall be devoted to your service and the service of our great Imperial Commonwealth to which we all belong "

Left
The Queen's Engagement 1947

Right
HM The Queen and HRH The Duke of Edinburgh's wedding in 1947

Innogy congratulates
Her Majesty the Queen
on her Golden Jubilee
Innogy is a leading integrated UK energy company. We generate electricity and, through our retail business npower, supply electricity, gas and other services to both the domestic and commercial markets. We also operate and manage power stations and run our own trading business.
Innogy plc
Windmill Hill
Business Park
Whitehill Way
Swindon
Wiltshire SN5 6PB
Telephone
01793 877777
Facsimile
01793 892525
Internet
www.innogy.com

But her father was not well. George VI was the fourth of Britain's twentieth century kings who would be brought down by smoking. He died at Sandringham in the small hours of February 6, 1952. This is the date from which Elizabeth II's accession, and hence her Golden Jubilee, has been dated, but it is a day which she herself, for fifty years, has treated as a time for mourning and memory of her beloved father. She stays at Sandringham and says prayers in a private memorial service in the bedroom where he died.

The new Queen herself was, famously, up a tree in Africa at the moment of her accession, observing the wildlife from the renowned Treetops Hotel in Kenya. It was a brief break from a tour which her father had been scheduled to make, before his health had deteriorated. When the news of the King's death finally reached Africa, it was Philip who broke the news to his wife. "He took her up to the garden," remembers Philip's aide, Michael Parker. "And they walked slowly up and down the lawn while he talked and talked and talked to her."

One of Elizabeth II's first decisions as Queen was that her Coronation, set for 2 June 1953, should not be televised. While she was happy for the ceremony to be recorded by film, which could be edited, the idea of live television made her nervous. When the ban became public in October 1952, the country blamed her venerable Prime Minister, Winston Churchill, and the popular outcry led by Fleet Street prompted the ban's removal. It was the first of several occasions in the next five decades when strongly voiced newspaper sentiment would dictate a dramatic switch of royal direction, and it set the stage for one of the great themes of Elizabeth II's reign – the shifting balance of the love-hate relationship between the media and the monarchy.

Previous page
Princess Elizabeth is greeted by Winston Churchill on her return from Africa following the death of her father George VI. February 1952. (top)
Princess Elizabeth (left) with Wallace Simpson at the funeral of Edward VII. (below)

This page
Spectators all-night vigil on processional route: some bedded down for the night in the Mall whie others rigged up portable canopies to protect themselves from the rain. (above left)
Spectators taking up positions at the foot of Eros n Piccadilly Circus on the Coronation route to wait through the night. June 1953. (above right)
A line of movie cameras and tripods set up for the Coronation. June 1953. (right)

Previos page
Top - Queen Elizabeth II (right) wearing robes of state in the Throne Room at Buckingham Palace, on her Coronation day. Her maids of Honour are beside her.
Below Left - Queen Elizabeth II (left) with her husband The Duke of Edinburgh, Queen Elizabeth the Queen Mother and Princess Margaret Rose (centre) in the throne room of Buckingham Palace after her Coronation Ceremony.
Below middle - Queen Elizabeth II leaving Buckingham Palace for her Coronation at Westminster Abbey.
Below right - Queen Elizabeth II arriving at Westminster Abbey for her Coronation Ceremony.

This page
Top left - Queen Elizabeth II and Prince Philip make their way to Westminster Abbey in a gilded coach for the Queen's Coronation.
Bottom left - Queen Elizabeth II on the balcony of Buckingham Palace after her Coronation Ceremony with (left to right) Prince Charles, Princess Anne and The Prince Philip, Duke of Edinburgh.
Top right - Princess Elizabeth after her Coronation as Queen Elizabeth II on the balcony of Buckingham Palace with her husband Prince Philip, acknowledges the cheers of the crowd gathered outside.
Bottom right - The canopy is placed over the Queen for the anointing ceremony during her Coronation.

Coronation of Queen Elizabeth II
at Westminster Abbey.

Previous page
Cockney's own party: 10 months earlier, Morpeth Street, in the East End of London, began collecting for Coronation Day. They raised £163 to give the children presents and to organize a street party in celebration of the occasion. (top)
A street party at Morpeth Street in London's East End to celebrate the Coronation of Queen Elizabeth II (below left)
A couple of East End boys blowing paper whistles at a street party held during Queen Elizabeth II's Coronation celebrations in London. (below right)

This page
Celebrations in Fulham (top).
The decorations in Fleet Street showing St Paul's Cathedral in the background. (below)

celebrate

the future's bright, the future's Orange

Orange makes a positive difference to people's lives by creating simple and innovative services that help people to communicate and interact better.

With operations currently in 20 countries across Europe and beyond, Orange aims to have a presence in markets covering 1.5 billion people worldwide by 2005.

To find out more about Orange around the world visit www.orange.com.

orange™

The Coronation itself was a triumph of ceremony and emotion. Despite herself, Elizabeth II was the star of Britain's first-ever televised mass-media event. It was followed by a triumphal six month tour of the Commonwealth in which vast crowds turned out to acclaim the beautiful young Queen who was being compared with Elizabeth I.

But, another running theme, the private life of her family, was becoming a source of public scandal. As her sister, Princess Margaret, left the Abbey on Coronation Day, she had playfully brushed a fleck of fluff from the uniform of Group Captain Peter Townsend, the war hero Comptroller of the Queen Mother's new household at Clarence House, and the secret of their romance was out. Townsend was divorced, conjuring up the dark shadows of the Abdication. For more than two years, until Margaret finally bowed to church and political pressure, her wish to marry her dashing Group Captain kept the newspapers at fever pitch.

Top left
Troops in the Mall.

Top right
A group of peers hurrying through the rain after the Coronation ceremony.

Middle right
Queen Mother at Coronation of Queen Elizabeth II with Prince Charles (?and Princess Margaret?)

Bottom right
The Royal group in the throne room of Buckingham Palace in honour of Coronation of Queen Elizabeth II, including the Duke of Edinburgh, Prince Charles, Princess Anne, the Queen Mother, Princess Margaret, the Duke of Gloucester, the Duchess of Gloucester, and the Duchess of Kent.

Fifty glorious years

FF
&P

Press scrutiny switched within years to rumoured trouble inside the Queen's own marriage, when Philip's absence on a tour of the South Pacific kept husband and wife apart for five months. The Queen's response to the rumours was to make a public statement praising her husband for his support of her work and to mark her gratitude by bestowing upon him the title of Prince of the United Kingdom. Philip had forfeited his Greek royal titles on becoming a British citizen in 1947. A few years later the couple started their second family, with Prince Andrew being born in 1960, followed by Edward in 1964.

With tricycles in the palace corridors, the 1960s saw the happiest period of the Queen's family life. "Mabel's Night Off" — the night when nanny Mabel Anderson surrendered her the nursery — was the high spot of the Queen's week, and the arrival towards the end of the decade of her eccentric mother-in-law, Princess Alice of Greece, in her grey nun's habit, added an exotic tinge to the extended domestic mix. In 1969 some flavour of this cheerful informality was captured by the ground-breaking television documentary, Royal Family, which revealed a relaxed and humorous Queen that the world had never seen. In private, Elizabeth II is a gifted mimic. She has brought family gatherings to their knees with her wicked imitations of her more pompous prime ministers — and she also performs a graphic imitation of Concorde, whose take-offs and landings are one of the modern drawbacks to life in Windsor Castle.

After a quarter of a century on the throne her Silver Jubilee in 1977 was an unexpected success. Britain was in the depths of economic misfortune, with galloping inflation and austerity measures dictated by the International Monetary Fund. But respect for the quiet and solid application of the Queen brought vast crowds onto the streets of London, and inspired more than twelve thousand street parties in every corner of the land.

Princess Elizabeth and Prince Charles, 1949.

Top left
Queen Elizabeth II watches her son Charles playing in a miniature car in the grounds of Balmoral Castle, Scotland. September 1952.

Middle left
Queen Elizabeth II with Princess Anne, Prince Charles and their nurse, Helen Lightbody, at a stall during a Sale of Work event in Abergeldie Castle, near Balmoral Castle in Aberdeenshire. They are raising funds for the building of a new vestry at Craithie Church. August 1955.

Right
The Royal family at lunch. 1968.

The Queen with her daughter-in-law The Princess of Wales at a charity polo match at Windsor in May 1997.

Insert left
The Golden State coach seen in use during the Jubilee celebrations in 1977.

Insert right
The Queen and Nelson Mandela travel to Buckingham Palace in an open landau during his State visit in 1996

With the post-Jubilee years, a new royal generation came to the forefront. The world was first enchanted, then horrified by the dramas of Charles and Diana, with Andrew, Fergie, and the princesses Anne and Margaret adding their own touches to the unfolding pattern of scandal. Prince Philip's outspoken "gaffes" added to the controversy that brought Royal popularity to an all-time low in the early 1990s. But through it all, respect for the Queen, and for her indomitable mother, remained constant. Critics spoke disparagingly of Elizabeth II's "dysfunctional" family, but her defenders pointed out how the long separations from her children, which may have been a factor in their later problems, derived from the arduous tours of foreign duty which were then considered part of her job.

The second quarter century of Elizabeth II's reign has seen some of her greatest triumphs. Abroad, she carried out her epoch-making state visits to China and to the democratic Russian Republic that marked the new, post cold war, world order. In Britain, she welcomed Nelson Mandela, the first black president of South Africa, in his historic state visit of July, 1996. The ending of apartheid and the coming of democracy to South Africa owed much to the pressure exerted by the Commonwealth — which, in turn, owed its own improbable survival in no small measure to the enduring faith of the Queen. British prime ministers might ignore the old imperial family of nations in favour of Europe, but the Queen saw no reason why both should not co-exist, and at some crucial moments her obstinate allegiance to the oath of service that she swore to the Commonwealth back in 1947 helped keep the institution afloat.

This page
Windsor Castle on fire in November 1992

Insert bottom
The Queen makes her famous 'annus horriblis' speech at the Guildhall, London in 1992.

Next page
The Queen and members of her family including Prince William and Prince Harry leave St. Paul's Cathedral, London after a service of celebration for the Queen Mother's 100th birthday in 2000.

Domestically, she and her advisors have seamlessly modernised the monarchy in many little-realised ways. The reforms of Lord Airlie, who brought management consultants into the Palace, produced changes which, from 1992, have cut royal expenditure on a yearly basis and made the monarchy one of the most efficient of Britain's official institutions. With its detailed annual accounts, it is certainly the most open. The Windsor Fire of 1992 led to the annual summer opening of Buckingham Palace, which not only paid for the repairs to Windsor Castle but has enabled visitors to inspect the grandeur and simplicity with which the world's most polished head-of-state organisation operates.

At the age of seventy-six, the Queen heads and personally supervises this historic British asset with undiminished verve, and with the coming of a new millennium, her sensitively conservative interpretation of her role is proving to have enduring appeal. Cool Britannia has come and gone, and Buckingham Palace remains the icon of Britishness. Witness the recent funeral of the Queen Mother. It is easy to satirise the red-tunicked guardsmen — until they stand to attention after a moment of international tragedy and play the American national anthem. As ex-President Bill Clinton put it, "You can't imagine what hearing the Queen's band play The Star-Spangled Banner meant to Americans."

The drama of September 11 showed the Queen's role — and also the Queen herself — at its best. Within two hours of the twin towers being hit, the Queen had issued a personal statement of sympathy, and plans were being laid for the service of remembrance at St Paul's Cathedral a few days later. Brushing away a tear as she spoke to bereaved relatives after the service, the Queen was the focus and embodiment of Britain's feelings at that moment — and this quiet, restrained, and thoroughly dutiful lady also spoke to a wider world.

A Very Personal *Tribute*

By Gyles Brandreth

The Queen and I go back a long way - all my life, in fact. That's the point, of course. For people of my generation, born just over half a century ago, the story of the Queen's reign has been the story of our lives.

In 1953, the Brandreth household acquired its first television set in order to be able to watch the Coronation 'live', and for the past forty-nine years I have continued watching the pageantry of monarchy, the rituals of royalty, and, latterly, the soap opera of the Royal Family, as they have flickered, at first in shaky black and white, eventually in glorious colour, on the small screen in the corner of the room.

Most of us know most of what we know about the Queen from what we have read in newspapers and magazines and seen on the box. Over the past twenty-five years, since the Silver Jubilee of 1977, I have been privileged to get glimpses of Her Majesty at closer quarters, through my work as a journalist, through my involvement with the National Playing Fields Association (the Queen is the charity's Patron, Prince Philip its President), and through my time as a member of parliament and a Lord Commissioner of Her Majesty's Treasury.

Queen Elizabeth II wearing the Imperial State Crown on the balcony of Buckingham Palace after her return in State Procession from her Coronation at Westminster Abbey. June 1953.

One of the Lords Commissioners' duties is to sign the government's cheques. I was intrigued to discover that with the larger amounts of national expenditure the Queen also signs the mandate. We once jointly signed a cheque for £96 billion (£ 96,861,662,000 to be precise!) As, nervously, I penned my name under Her Majesty's signature for the first time, I could not help wondering why two signatures were required. Which of the pair of us did the government not trust?

The more I have seen the Queen in action the more I have admired her. The more cynical and less deferential our society has become, the more fragile and less secure the monarchy's automatic hold on the affection and loyalty of the public at large has become, the more my respect for the person of the monarch has grown. I am a fan of Queen Elizabeth II. Why? I could give you fifty reasons, but I will settle for five or six.

First, I admire her dedication, her commitment, her absolute and sustained acceptance of the bizarre role fate threw her way. Famously, on her twenty-first birthday, April 26 1947, in a broadcast from South Africa to the United Kingdom, Commonwealth and Empire, she made public what she described as a 'solemn act of dedication': 'I declare before you all that my whole life, whether it be long or short, shall be devoted to your service and the service of the great imperial family to which we all belong.' Others might kick against the pricks - possibly Prince Philip in the 1950s; probably the Prince of Wales, off and on, in his darker moments; certainly, Diana, Princess of Wales, as we all know - but the Queen has never baulked at her obligations, never moaned about her lot. Having made her promise, she has kept her word.

This page
Top. The Queen and members of her family at the Trooping of the Colour in 1985.
Center. The Queen with some of her family at a press photo call held at Sandringham in 1987.
Bottom. The Queen, Prince William and Prince Harry at St. Paul's cathedral, London in July 2000.

Opposite
The Queen with three generations of her family as they leave church after the Christmas Day service, Sandringham, Norfolk. 1991.

Next, I admire her style. I don't mean her look. I am no judge of fashion. I mean the way she is true to herself. The Queen has the interests, attributes and tastes of an English (or Scottish) countrywoman of her class and generation. Dogs and horses (and racing form) she knows and understands. She does not pretend to be what she is not. She will attend the Royal Variety Performance and, even, if it cannot be avoided, a rock concert or the opera, but we know that, in her heart, she is happiest following wholly traditional country pursuits. She may be apolitical, but she is not one for political correctness. If she chooses, she will go out riding without a hard hat, she will happily wear a fur coat, and in her assorted residences cigarettes are freely available to her guests.

Thirdly, I admire her ability to keep at it, year in, year out, to repeat the relentless routine. When I was MP for the City of Chester, in the spring of 1992 the Queen came to Chester Cathedral for the Royal Maundy service. It was a memorable occasion, unique for most of us who were there. For the Queen, of course, it was simply what she always does on the Thursday before Easter. There is an alarming predictability to her diary. Her year barely varies: Sandringham for the New Year, Windsor Castle for Ascot, Holyroodhouse in July, Balmoral for the summer, Buckingham Palace when Parliament is sitting. If you are honoured at an invesituture, it is a special moment for you, and the Queen helps make it so, but there are up to twenty-two investitures each year (and at least four garden parties, often more) and, as far as the Queen is concerned, their shape and scope, and the courteous, friendly, small-talk required at every one of them, never varies.

This page
Top. Badminton Horse Trials, April 1980
Center. The Queen and Prince of Wales at the Epsom races in June 1993.
Bottom. At Sandringham Church, Norfolk, August 1985, celebrating the Queen Mother's 85th birthday.

Opposite
Off duty and dressed casually. The Queen and Queen Mother join the spectators at the Badminton Horse Trials in April 1978.

This year is very much like last year and next year will be much the same. It would drive most of us to the brink. The Queen simply takes it in her stride. Of course, the Queen does get to meet people and go to places you and I might not. There have been more than eighty state visits to the United Kingdom since the Queen's accession (King Gustav VI of Sweden and Emperor Hailie Selassie of Ethiopia were the first to call), and a similar number of state visits paid to other countries by the Queen and Prince Philip, but, while the personnel changes and the backdrops differ, there is an essential unforgiving sameness about the management and execution of state affairs. For the Queen, the novelty of her life must have worn off many years ago.

I also admire Her Majesty's dogged commitment to the Commonwealth. When her reign began, the Empire was already embarked on its inevitable decline and the Commonwealth as we know it still in its infancy. In 1952, there were eight members of the Commonwealth. Today, there are fifty-four, of which sixteen are still constitutional monarchies with the Queen as head of state. These days Whitehall and Westminster may be preoccupied with the United Kingdom's relations with Europe and the United States, but the Queen has never been a dedicated follower of fashion. There is nothing sexy about the Commonwealth, but that does not trouble Her Majesty. Her deep-seated interest in, and knowledgeable enthusiasm for, what she describes as a 'free and voluntary association of equal partners' that 'in all history has no precedent' is a wonder to behold.

Top
The Queen and Prince of Wales seen at a polo match at the Guards Polo Club, Windsor in June 1997.

I admire her discretion. The Queen has never given an interview and I hope she never will. We can have all the tittle-tattle we want (and rather more) about her immediate family and her in-laws, but the Queen is the Sovereign and a certain mystery becomes her. Yes, we know she is intelligent, shrewd, well-informed. I have spoken with five prime ministers who can testify on that score. They all say, even off the record, even in their cups, that she is unfailingly well-briefed, up to speed and perceptive. It is equally evident to all who have met her that she has a playful sense of humour, but is fundamentally a serious individual, a committed Christian, with a profound sense of duty and responsibility.

I remember attending the lunch at Guildhall in the City of London to mark the fortieth anniversary of her accession. When she arrived, it was obvious she had a filthy cold. She said, 'I am going to make my speech before lunch because otherwise I don't think my voice will last, and I want to be heard.' That was the occasion of the 'annus horribilis' speech, when she looked back on 1992, the year when part of Windsor Castle was destroyed by fire and the first marriages of all three of her elder children went up in smoke as well. In that speech, she gave us a glimpse of the heartache that would affect any mother under such circumstances, but there was nothing self-pitying or self-indulgent about it. The Queen is not a touchy-feely monarch and I am grateful for that.

Main picture
The Queen and Prince Philip seen in Arromanche, France during the D.Day Commemorations in May 1994.

Inset
The Queen and family members wave off the bride and groom – The Earl and Countess of Wessex after their marriage at St. George's Chapel, Windsor in July 1999.

Opposite Page
The Queen, hardly recognisable, as she inspects fire damage to Windsor Castle in 1992.

Top
The Queen and Princess of Wales travel to the state opening of parliament in 1983.

Bottom
The Queen and members of her family attend the Trooping of the Colour in June 2000.

While the Queen, very sensibly, does not talk to the press, I have interviewed the Duke of Edinburgh a couple of times. He spoke to me readily about his own work, his philosophy of life, his children, even his sometime daughters-in-law, but when it came to the Queen, his role as her consort, his attitude to her achievement, he clammed up. His commitment to the Queen is absolute - and not to be discussed. But if you press him on the virtue that the Queen displays most in her dealings with her family and the world - indeed the virtue that is also essential to a successful marriage - he says: 'The Queen has the quality of tolerance in abundance.'

Dedicated, dutiful, discreet, tolerant, she has barely put a foot wrong in fifty years. (I know politicians who can barely keep out of trouble for fifty minutes.) And she has a dazzling smile. These days, when her face is in repose, she can look quite fearsome, even grumpy, but when she smiles the effect is extraordinary. On the fortieth anniversary of her accession, on February 6 1992, she began the day at a church service at Sandringham and then went on to visit cancer patients at a local hospital. Recently, in the run-up to her Golden Jubilee, I accompanied the Queen when she went to visit other cancer patients at St Luke's Hospice in Harrow.

As we toured the wards, it was fascinating to see at close quarters the effect of that dazzling smile. In the final bed was an elderly patient, whose cancer had robbed him of the power of speech. His wife explained that he came originally from Kenya, from Nairobi. 'Kenya is a beautiful country,' said the Queen. 'Yes,' said the patient's wife, 'When you came in 1952 we were there, in the streets, waving flags.' 'Were you?' said the Queen, suddenly looking quite solemn, 'I remember it, of course. My visit was cut short, sadly, when the King died.' There was a long pause and then the Queen looked again at the man lying in the bed and smiled. He was scribbling furiously on a notepad. Eventually, he passed what he had written to the Queen. She fumbled in her handbag for her glasses. She couldn't find them, so I read the man's message out loud: 'Thank you for coming to see me, Your Majesty. This has been the happiest and proudest day of my life.' And he meant it.

Golden Jubilee Programme of *Events*

The first Prime Minister of The Queen's reign was Winston Churchill

An overview of The Queen's reign

by the Royal web editor, Buckingham Palace

The Queen's reign began unexpectedly on an ordinary Wednesday in 1952. King George VI, The Queen's father, died suddenly at Sandringham on February 6 after several years of ill health. The news of his death reached 25-year-old Princess Elizabeth in the afternoon of that day in Kenya, where the Princess and Prince Philip had just begun a Commonwealth tour. Having left Britain a Princess, she was to return as Queen.

Upon the news of King George's death, the Royal party flew back to Britain, arriving at London Airport the next day after a 4,600 mile journey. The new Queen was met by Winston Churchill, the prime minister, and Anthony Eden, the Foreign Secretary. Following the funeral of King George VI and the 16-week period of Court mourning, there was opportunity for national celebration with the coronation of Queen Elizabeth II in Westminster Abbey on 2 June 1953.

From the earliest days, The Queen took up her new role with energetic commitment.

Political duties began immediately, from the State Opening of Parliament to weekly audiences with the prime minister. The first prime minister of The Queen's reign was Winston Churchill. The Queen also had occasion to exercise her Royal prerogative, appointing Harold Macmillan as Prime Minister in 1957. At that time, the Conservative Party did not have any formal electoral machinery to choose a new leader, and The Queen acted on the advice of government ministers. It was a role which was to arise again in 1963.

Date	Event	Location
27 Apr	Rolls Royce and Bentley cars parade, Windsor.	Windsor
29 Apr	The Queen and The Duke of Edinburgh attend a Dinner hosted by the Prime Minister	London
30 Apr	The Queen accompanied by The Duke of Edinburgh will address both Houses of Parliament	London
1 May	The Queen accompanied by The Duke of Edinburgh to visit Truro Cathedral	Truro
1 May	The Queen accompanied by The Duke of Edinburgh, will view a Celebration of Cornish Gardens	Truro
1 May	The Queen accompanied by The Duke of Edinburgh, will visit the National Maritime Museum	Falmouth
1 May	The Queen, and The Duke of Edinburgh, will attend a performance at Exeter Cathedral and a reception.	Exeter
2 May	The Queen and The Duke of Edinburgh will visit Wells	Wells
2 May	The Queen will visit Farmers' Market and Vivary Park in Taunton.	Taunton
2 May	The Queen, accompanied by The Duke of Edinburgh will attend Lunch at Guildhall, Bath	Bath
2 May	The Queen, accompanied by The Duke of Edinburgh, will attend a reception at the Pump Rooms, Bath.	Bath
2 May	The Queen, accompanied by The Duke of Edinburgh, will view Bath Abbey restoration.	Bath
7 May	The Queen accompanied by The Duke of Edinburgh will attend a Gala event at City Hall, Newcastle.	Newcastle upon Tyne
7 May	The Queen accompanied by The Duke of Edinburgh, will visit the Baltic Centre, Gateshead.	Gateshead
7 May	The Queen and The Duke of Edinburgh will open Metro Link	Sunderland
7 May	The Queen will visit St. Joseph's Roman Catholic Primary School.	Jarrow

The Queen took her role as Queen of the whole of the United Kingdom seriously. She began a wide-ranging programme of visits throughout every part of the country. Her first regional tour was a three-day visit to Northern Ireland. In the same decade The Queen travelled north, south, east and west, from Shetland to the Isles of Scilly, and from Swansea to Holy Island.

Taking her duties as Head of the Commonwealth seriously, The Queen embarked on a series of overseas visits through every part of the realms and Commonwealth. Within the first few years of her reign, The Queen travelled to parts of the Commonwealth never before visited by her predecessors. The Queen also represented Britain in State Visits to countries including Norway, Sweden, Portugal, France, Denmark, the USA and the Netherlands.

Family life remained an essential stay throughout official duties. As well as being Sovereign, The Queen was a mother and had to care for two young children. With the birth of Prince Andrew in 1960, The Queen became the first reigning Sovereign to give birth since Queen Victoria, who had her youngest child, Princess Beatrice, in 1857.

Date	Event	Location
7 May	The Queen, accompanied by The Duke of Edinburgh, will open Winter Gardens, Sunderland.	Sunderland
7 May	The Queen, and The Duke of Edinburgh will open the Millennium Bridge at Gateshead.	Gateshead
8 May	The Queen accompanied by The Duke of Edinburgh will visit Darlington.	Darlington
8 May	The Queen accompanied by The Duke of Edinburgh will visit Blackhall Rocks.	Peterlee
8 May	The Queen accompanied by The Duke of Edinburgh will visit Easington	Peterlee
8 May	The Queen accompanied by The Duke of Edinburgh will visit Seaham, County Durham.	Seaham
8 May	The Queen, accompanied by The Duke of Edinburgh, will open Millennium Place, Durham.	Durham
8 May	The Queen, accompanied by The Duke of Edinburgh, will visit Durham Castle	Durham
9 May	The Queen accompanied by The Duke of Edinburgh will vist East London.	London
9 May	Visit to Barking by The Queen and The Duke of Edinburgh	Barking
9 May	Visit to Redbridge by The Queen and The Duke of Edinburgh	Redbridge
9 May	Visit to Waltham Forest by The Queen and The Duke of Edinburgh	London
9 May	Visit to West Ham United Football Ground in Newham by The Queen	London
10 May	The Queen will visit Aylesbury.	Aylesbury
10 May	The Queen, accompanied by The Duke of Edinburgh, will visit Bisham Abbey.	Marlow
10 May	The Queen, accompanied by The Duke of Edinburgh, will visit Higginson Park	Marlow
16 - 17 May	The Queen will attend The Royal Windsor Horse Show.	Windsor
18 May	The Queen will take the Salute at "All The Queen's Horses", Royal Windsor Horse Show	Windsor

As well as being Sovereign, The Queen was a mother and had to care for two young children

The second decade of The Queen's reign saw the introduction of further innovations to make the work of the monarchy accessible to an even wider range of people. During their visit to Australia and New Zealand in 1970, for example, The Queen and The Duke of Edinburgh initiated a new practice - the 'walkabout' - to allow them to meet as many people as possible. There was also increased access for the media. In 1969 the first television film about the family life of the Royal Family was shown. 'Royal Family' was watched by 23 million viewers and included footage of the off-duty activities of The Queen and her family.

Another innovation was the opening in 1962 of a new gallery at Buckingham Palace to display items from the Royal Collection. The brainchild of The Duke of Edinburgh, the new Queen's Gallery occupied the space of the Palace's bomb-damaged private chapel. It was the first time that parts of the Palace had been opened to the general public, and proved very popular. In politics, the issue of The Queen's Royal prerogative in politics arose again in 1963, as it had done in 1957. Following the retirement of Harold Macmillan, The Queen acted on the advice of Macmillan in appointing Lord Home as Prime Minister and leader of the Conservative party. The choice caused some controversy, and in 1965 the Conservatives instituted an electoral procedure by which to decide the Party's leadership in the future. The Queen has played no role in the election of Conservative Party leaders subsequently.

Date	Event	Location
20 May	The Queen will visit the Chelsea Flower Show	London
21 May	The Queen will open the new Queen's Gallery at Buckingham Palace.	London
22 May	The Queen will attend a Royal Academies evening at the Royal Academy, London.	London
23 May	The Queen, and The Duke of Edinburgh, will attend a Thanksgiving Service at Glasgow Cathedral.	Glasgow
24 May	The Queen will give a Reception in the Palace of Holyroodhouse.	Edinburgh
24 May	The Queen, accompanied by The Duke of Edinburgh, will open Falkirk Wheel at Millennium Link.	Falkirk
25 May	The Queen will host a Garden Party at the Palace of Holyroodhouse.	Edinburgh
26 May	The Queen will attend General Assembly of the Church of Scotland, Edinburgh	Edinburgh
27 May	The Queen accompanied by The Duke of Edinburgh will visit the Isle of Skye.	Isle of Skye
27 May	The Queen and The Duke of Edinburgh will attend a Lunch at Stornoway.	Stornoway
27 May	The Queen and The Duke of Edinburgh will attend a Tea Party at Wick.	Wick
27 May	The Queen and The Duke of Edinburgh will visit Caithness.	Caithness
27 May	The Queen and The Duke of Edinburgh will visit the Isle of Lewis.	Isle of Lewis
28 May	The Queen will attend a reception at City Chambers, Dundee.	Dundee
28 May	The Queen, accompanied by The Duke of Edinburgh, will open The Space, School of Dance.	Dundee
28 May	The Queen, accompanied by The Duke of Edinburgh, will visit 'Aberdeen - Our City'	Aberdeen
28 May	The Queen, accompanied by The Duke of Edinburgh, will visit City Chambers, Dundee.	Dundee

In 1969 the first television film about the family life of the Royal Family was shown and included footage of the off-duty activities of The Queen and her family

Prince Charles and Princess Anne began to undertake their first Royal duties in support of their parents' work

The Queen made several historic overseas visits, including the first visit by a monarch to West Germany since the war. In the divided city of West Berlin, The Queen surveyed the Berlin Wall. Other members of the Royal Family attended the independence ceremonies of countries formerly in the British Empire, subsequently giving rise to the Commonwealth.

The Queen and The Duke of Edinburgh had a new addition to their family with a fourth child, Prince Edward, in 1964. Prince Charles and Princess Anne began to undertake their first Royal duties in support of their parents' work. Prince Charles' role as heir to the throne was formally acknowledged when The Queen invested him as Prince of Wales in a ceremony at Caernafon in 1969. The ceremony was watched on television by 200 million people worldwide.

The third decade of The Queen's reign included a number of milestone events, causes for public and private celebration. In 1977 The Queen marked twenty-five years as Sovereign. The Silver Jubilee was met with a nationwide tour, Commonwealth visits and celebrations at every level. The Queen and The Duke of Edinburgh travelled 56,000 miles in total to mark the occasion in as many parts of the United Kingdom and Commonwealth as possible.

Date	Event	Location
28 May	The Queen, and The Duke of Edinburgh, will visit Scottish Parliament, sitting at King's College.	Aberdeen
29 May	The Queen and The Duke of Edinburgh will attend a Borders Gathering at Melrose Rugby Club	Melrose
29 May	The Queen and The Duke of Edinburgh will visit Lauder.	Melrose
29 May	The Queen, accompanied by The Duke of Edinburgh, will visit Melrose Abbey.	Melrose
29 May	The Queen, and The Duke of Edinburgh, will attend lunch hosted by the Scottish Borders Council.	Melrose
1 Jun	The Queen will host a Classical Concert in the Gardens at Buckingham Palace.	London
2 Jun	The Queen will attend a Jubilee Church Service at St. George's Chapel, Windsor Castle.	Windsor
3 Jun	The Queen accompanied by The Duke of Edinburgh will attend events in Slough.	Slough
3 Jun	The Queen accompanied by The Duke of Edinburgh will attend events in Windsor.	Windsor
3 Jun	The Queen will host a Pop Concert in the Gardens at Buckingham Palace, and will light a Beacon.	London
4 Jun	Ceremonial Procession to St Paul's Cathedral where The Queen will attend a Thanksgiving service.	London
4 Jun	The Queen will attend a lunch hosted by the Lord Mayor and the Corporation of London at Guildhall	London
4 Jun	The Queen will make a Balcony Appearance at Buckingham Palace and watch a Royal Air Force Fly Past.	London
4 Jun	The Queen, and The Duke of Edinburgh, will attend the Golden Jubilee Festival in The Mall.	London
6 Jun	The Queen accompanied by The Duke of Edinburgh will visit North London.	London
6 Jun	The Queen will attend a garden party at Lambeth Palace.	London

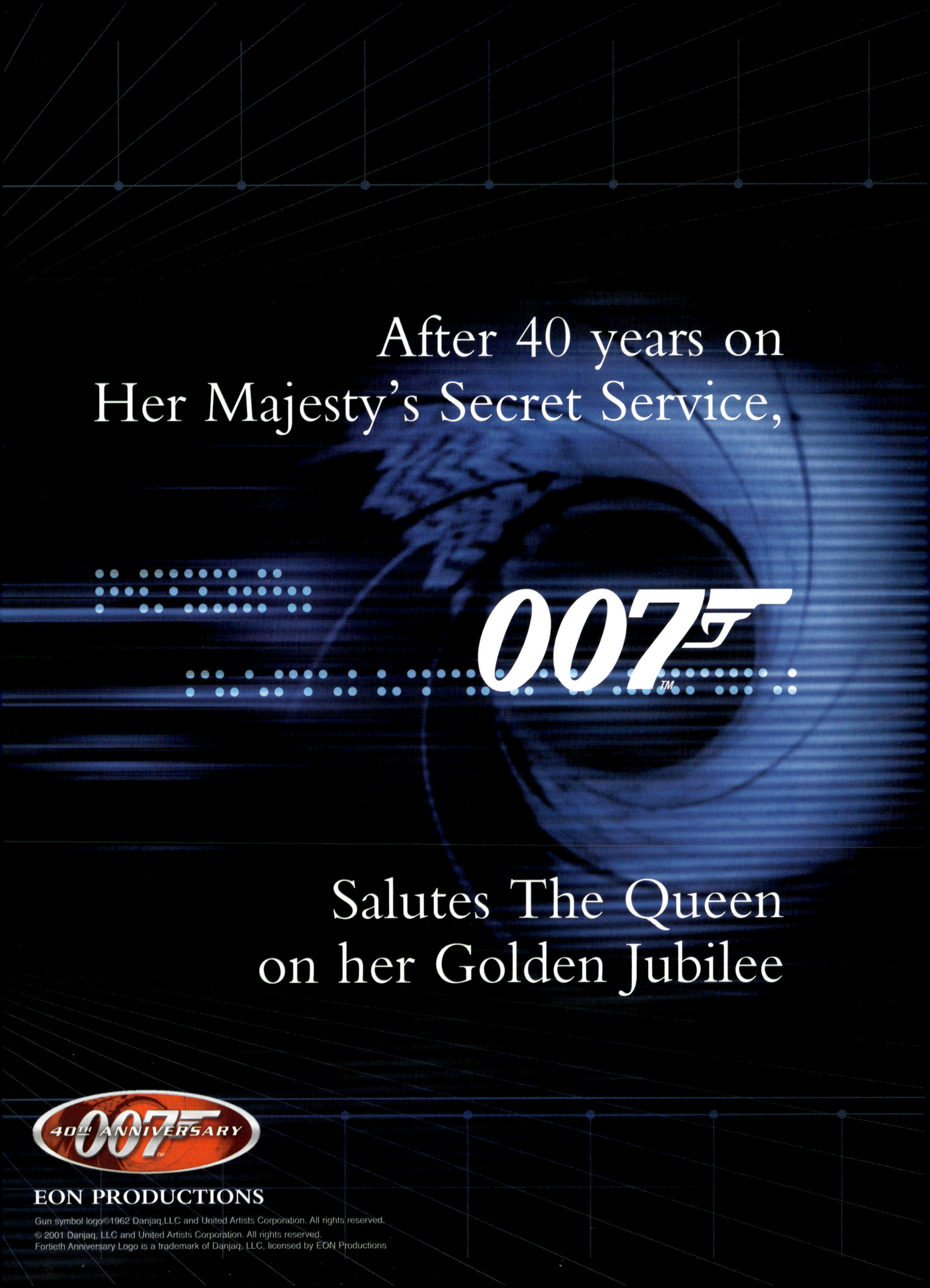
After 40 years on
Her Majesty's Secret Service,
007
Salutes The Queen
on her Golden Jubilee
40th ANNIVERSARY 007
EON PRODUCTIONS
Gun symbol logo©1962 Danjaq,LLC and United Artists Corporation. All rights reserved.
© 2001 Danjaq, LLC and United Artists Corporation. All rights reserved.
Fortieth Anniversary Logo is a trademark of Danjaq, LLC, licensed by EON Productions

The Queen and Duke of Edinburgh celebrated 25 years of marriage in 1972

The weddings of Princess Anne to Captain Mark Phillips (1973) and The Prince of Wales to Lady Diana Spencer (1981) were also cause for widespread public rejoicing. The Queen and Duke of Edinburgh themselves celebrated 25 years of marriage in 1972 with a service of thanksgiving at Westminster Abbey. In 1977 they had their first grandchild, with the birth of a son, Peter, to Princess Anne.

The decade had its share of personal grief. The Queen's uncle, The Duke of Windsor and former King Edward VIII, died in Paris on 28 May 1972 at the age of 77. The Queen's 30-year-old cousin, Prince William of Gloucester, was killed in 1972 in a flying accident, as a result of which The Queen cancelled her visit to the Munich Olympics. In 1979 Earl Mountbatten of Burma was assassinated by an IRA bomb blast while the Earl was fishing in Co Sligo, Eire. Cousin to The Queen and uncle to The Duke of Edinburgh, Earl Mountbatten was First Sea Lord and Chief of the Defence Staff; he had also been the last Viceroy of India before independence.

The Queen's political duties continued as usual. In 1974, The Queen had to fly back from an Australian tour when a general election was suddenly called - it is the only time she has done so. Following the general election in February, no one party had a clear majority in the House of Commons. The question arose as to whether The Queen should endorse a coalition between the Conservative and the Liberal parties without first giving Labour, the largest party, a chance to form a government. The Tories and Liberals were, in the end, unable to arrange a coalition, and Harold Wilson returned to power as Prime Minister.

Date	Event	Location
6 Jun	Visit to Barnet by The Queen and The Duke of Edinburgh	London
6 Jun	Visit to Brent The Queen and The Duke of Edinburgh	Wembley
6 Jun	Visit to Haringey by The Queen and The Duke of Edinburgh.	London
7 Jun	The Queen will attend the South of England Show, Ardingly, West Sussex.	Ardingly
10 Jun	The Queen, and The Duke of Edinburgh, will host a Multifaith Reception at Buckingham Palace.	London
11 Jun	The Queen accompanied by The Duke of Edinburgh will lunch at Penrhyn Castle	Penrhyn
11 Jun	The Queen will attend a sports event at Colwyn Bay in Wales.	Colwyn Bay
11 Jun	The Queen will attend a thanksgiving service at Bangor Cathedral.	Bangor
11 Jun	The Queen will visit a crafts exhibition and fair at Beaumaris Castle.	Beaumaris
11 Jun	The Queen, accompanied by The Duke of Edinburgh, will arrive at Llanfairpwll Railway Station.	Llanfairpwll
12 Jun	The Queen accompanied by The Duke of Edinburgh will attend a Lunch in Carmarthenshire	Carmarthen
12 Jun	The Queen accompanied by The Duke of Edinburgh will open the Millennium Coastal Park,	Llanelli
12 Jun	The Queen accompanied by The Duke of Edinburgh will visit the Carmarthenshire Enterprise Day	Llanelli
12 Jun	The Queen will attend Powys picnic, Dolau.	Landrindod Wells
12 Jun	The Queen will attend a Festival of Youth and Community Service, Margram Park.	Port Talbot
12 Jun	The Queen will open improvement works and a new lock at Burry Port Harbour.	Carmarthen
13 Jun	The Queen will attend Welcome to the Valleys at Treorchi, Rhondda Valley.	Tonypandy
13 Jun	The Queen will drive through the shopping centre of Bridgend	Bridgend

THE QUEEN'S GOLDEN JUBILEE 2002

PONTIN'S

would like to offer their congratulations to Her Majesty the Queen on her Golden Jubilee 1952 – 2002

In 1952, when Her Majesty the Queen ascended to the throne, Pontin's had already been providing holidays for six years. Over the fifty years of her reign, many things have changed and none more so than at the original camps which have developed over time into the modern family holiday centres of today.

Started in 1946 by Fred Pontin, who later became Sir Fred Pontin in 1977, Pontin's provided the ideal escape for thousands of British people who had suffered the hardships of the war years. His concept was a week's holiday for a week's pay which at that time was the princely sum of £7 full board. In those days the accommodation was basic, lavatories, baths and showers were housed in separate purpose built blocks and certain foods were rationed until 1954. Guests still enjoyed three meals a day and the company quickly developed the 'value for money' reputation which it is still famous for today.

During the difficult post war years, the young Queen played an important role in uniting the British people as they built new lives and moved forward to a brighter future.

In the 1960's, major changes in the British life-style began to emerge. Self-catering holidays began to become popular with Pontin's taking the initiative of developing the concept of holidays centres abroad and Pontinental was born.

Over the years corporate and private companies have owned and invested in the business, improved the accommodation, facilities and entertainment to meet the needs everchanging public tastes. Comfortable apartments await today's guests; a multitude of activities from abseiling to quad bikes, zip wires to aeroball keep the most active of children happy. Pontin's also hold a wide range of themed breaks from sport to music and dance with something on offer for all.

The holiday centre facilities may have come a long way from the original wooden chalets but what has not changed is the fun and enjoyment that visitors to the centres experience. Pontin's guests are still the same sociable, out going people who love to have a good time with the family, meeting old friends and making new ones.

Over the years the Queen has worked hard for this country and the Commonwealth. Her Majesty's dignity and dedication to duty has remained steadfast throughout her reign and has earned her respect throughout the world.

As Pontin's guests and staff celebrate this auspicious occasion, we will be wishing Her Majesty the Queen a very happy Golden Jubilee.

The Queen received the first female prime minister at Buckingham Palace, when Margaret Thatcher replaced James Callaghan as leader in 1979

Later in the decade, The Queen received the first female prime minister at Buckingham Palace, when Margaret Thatcher replaced James Callaghan as leader in 1979.

On the international stage, too, there were several 'firsts'. The Queen paid an historic visit to communist Yugoslavia in 1972, travelled to Japan as the guest of Emperor Hirohito in 1975, was the first British Sovereign to travel to the Middle East in 1979, and visited Pope John Paul II in the Vatican in 1980. The Commonwealth went from strength to strength. The Queen, as Head of the Commonwealth, visited Ottawa at the time of the Commonwealth Heads of Government Meeting. Since then The Queen has been present in the host country for every CHOGM, in Britain or abroad, to demonstrate her commitment to the organisation and its principles.

The vital service of the Armed Forces was a prominent theme throughout the fourth decade, with two conflicts involving UK servicemen and women. British troops travelled to the South Atlantic in April 1982 to recover the Falkland Islands and South Georgia. In addition to her usual concern for the Forces of which she is Head, The Queen shared the anxiety of many other mothers of men and women serving in the conflict. Prince Andrew was the pilot of a Sea King helicopter during the war.

In the second conflict, in January 1991, British forces travelled to the Gulf in the Middle East to assist in the Allied action to drive out Iraqi armies from occupied Kuwait. At the end of the decade, The Queen led the commemoration of an event in the Second World War - the 50th anniversary of the Battle of Britain.

Date	Event	Location
13 Jun	The Queen, accompanied by The Duke of Edinburgh, will visit the National Assembly for Wales.	Cardiff
13 Jun	The Queen, accompanied by The Duke of Edinburgh, attend Reception hosted by Cardiff City Council.	Cardiff
13 Jun	The Queen, accompanied by The Duke of Edinburgh, will attend a Lunch in Newport.	Newport
13 Jun	The Queen, accompanied by the Duke of Edinburgh, will visit Heritage Park, Porth.	Pontypridd
15 Jun	The Queen, and The Duke of Edinburgh, will attend The Queen's Birthday Parade, Horseguards	London
17 Jun	The Queen will host a dinner for European Sovereigns at Windsor Castle.	Windsor
17 Jun	The Queen, and The Duke of Edinburgh, will attend the Service of the Order of the Garter at Windsor.	Windsor
18 - 22 Jun	The Queen accompanied by The Duke of Edinburgh, will attend Royal Ascot.	Ascot
25 Jun	The Queen and The Duke of Edinburgh will visit West London.	London
25 Jun	Visit to Bushy Park by The Queen and The Duke of Edinburgh	Twickenham
25 Jun	Visit to Gunnersbury Park by The Queen and The Duke of Edinburgh	London
25 Jun	Visit to Hillingdon by The Queen and The Duke of Edinburgh.	Uxbridge
25 Jun	Visit to Kingston-upon-Thames by The Queen and The Duke of Edinburgh.	Kingston upon Thames
26 Jun	The Queen will host an Armed Forces Dinner at Windsor Castle.	Windsor
27 Jun	The Queen will visit Portsmouth.	Portsmouth
27 Jun	The Queen will visit the Armed Forces Portsmouth.	Portsmouth
2 Jul	The Queen will open Millennium Point Science and Learning Centre, Digbeth, Birmingham.	Birmingham

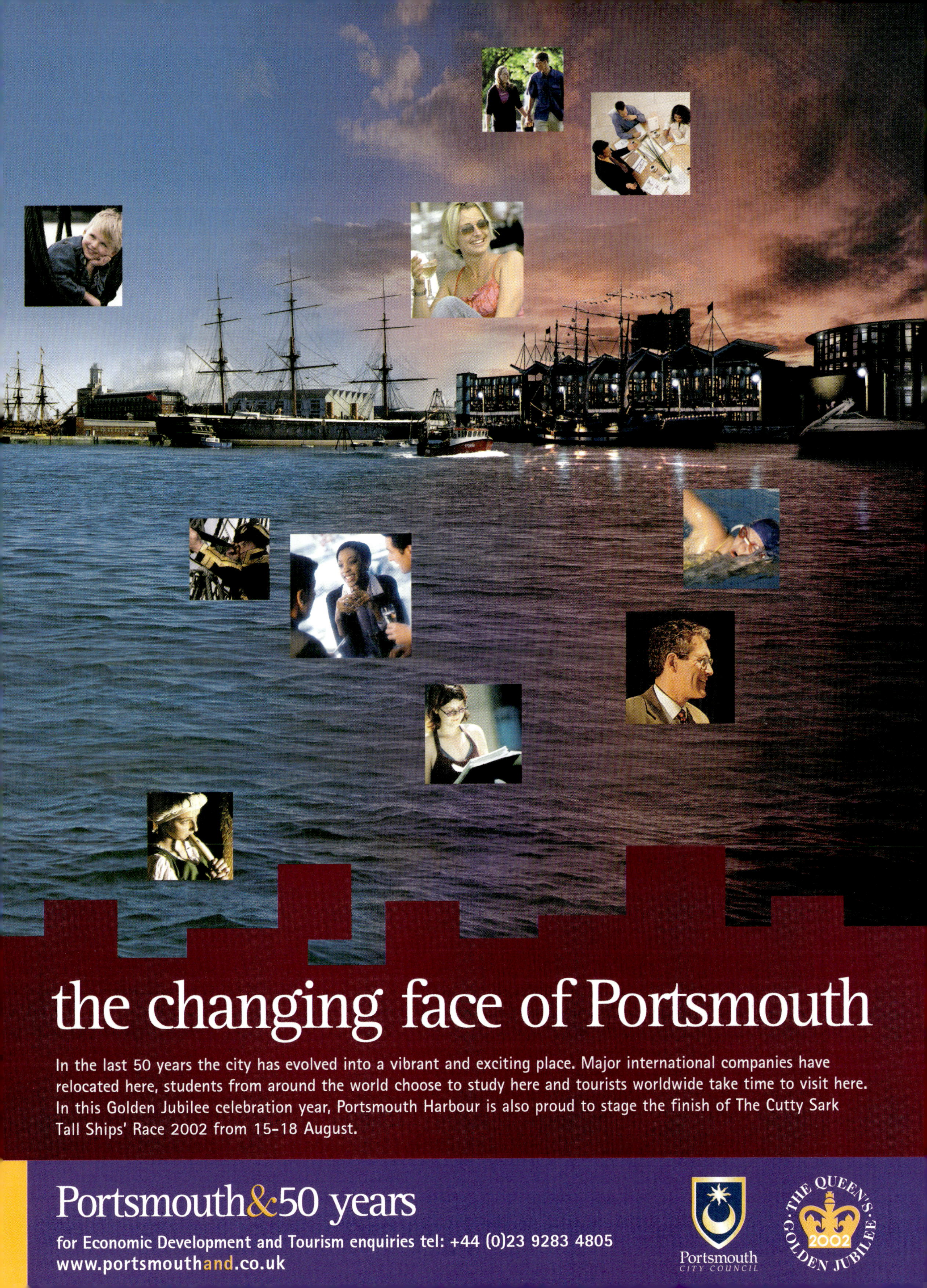
the changing face of Portsmouth
In the last 50 years the city has evolved into a vibrant and exciting place. Major international companies have relocated here, students from around the world choose to study here and tourists worldwide take time to visit here. In this Golden Jubilee celebration year, Portsmouth Harbour is also proud to stage the finish of The Cutty Sark Tall Ships' Race 2002 from 15-18 August.
Portsmouth&50 years
for Economic Development and Tourism enquiries tel: +44 (0)23 9283 4805
www.portsmouthand.co.uk
Portsmouth
CITY COUNCIL
THE QUEEN'S GOLDEN JUBILEE
2002

The decade also saw political and religious barriers being broken down in several important events. History was made in 1982 when Pope John Paul II visited Britain, the first pope to do so for 450 years. The Queen, titular Head of the Church of England, received him at Buckingham Palace, where the Pope promised to pray for the safe return of Prince Andrew from the South Atlantic. In the same decade The Queen and Prince Philip travelled to China, the first time in history that a British monarch had visited the country.

Ties with the Commonwealth were reinforced by visits to Australia, New Zealand, Canada and the Caribbean. They allowed The Queen to participate in key events in each country's political independence. In February 1983, The Queen opened the Jamaican Parliament in its 21st anniversary year of independence, and Australia's bicentenary year in 1988 was celebrated with visits by The Queen and Prince Philip as well as The Prince and Princess of Wales.

Date	Event	Location
2 Jul	The Queen, accompanied by The Duke of Edinburgh, will attend Reception and Concert in Symphony Hall.	Birmingham
2 Jul	The Queen, and The Duke of Edinburgh will visit Millennium Point Science & Learning Centre.	Birmingham
2 Jul	The Queen, and The Duke of Edinburgh will visit Touchwood, Solihull.	Solihull
3 Jul	The Queen, accompanied by The Duke of Edinburgh will visit Royal Show, Stoneleigh, Warwickshire.	Kenilworth
3 Jul	The Queen, accompanied by The Duke of Edinburgh, will visit Brewhouse Arts Centre.	Burton-on-Trent
3 Jul	The Queen, and The Duke of Edinburgh, will attend a National Museum of Brewing	Burton-upon-Trent
3 Jul	The Queen, and The Duke of Edinburgh, will visit the National Memorial Arboretum	Burton-on-Trent
4 Jul	The Queen and The Duke of Edinburgh will visit South London.	London
4 Jul	Visit to Croydon by The Queen and The Duke of Edinburgh	Croydon
4 Jul	Visit to Lewisham by The Queen and The Duke of Edinburgh	London
4 Jul	Visit to the London Youth Games at Crystal Palace by The Queen	Bromley
5 Jul	Parade for Her Majesty's body guards and the In-Pensioners of the Royal Hospital Chelsea	London
9 Jul	Garden Party for people born on Accession day.	London
9 Jul	Medal winners of The Queen's Golden Jubilee Poetry Competition.	London
11 Jul	The Queen accompanied by The Duke of Edinburgh will visit Harewood House, Leeds	Leeds
11 Jul	The Queen will meet The Queen's Golden Jubilee Baton Relay Runners.	Leeds

History was made in 1982 when Pope John Paul II visited Britain, the first pope to do so for 450 years

A major innovator for 50 years and more
BERTONE
www.michelin.co.uk

The Queen and Duke of Edinburgh had more grandchildren with the birth of two sons to The Prince and Princess of Wales and two daughters to The Duke and Duchess of York. Members of the Royal Family continued to support the work of The Queen in official royal work for a wide range of charities and organisations. They also travelled widely abroad as The Queen's representatives.

The fifth decade of The Queen's reign took her into a new century and the third millennium. The last ten years, as The Queen entered her seventies, saw little reduction in her duties, or in the workload of The Duke of Edinburgh.

The Queen has continued to exercise her constitutional role as Head of State - for example, by opening Parliament each session, holding audiences with the Prime Minister and other ministers, and receiving ambassadors. The decade saw constitutional history made in the United Kingdom when The Queen opened new devolved constitutional bodies for Scotland and Wales. In May 1999 The Queen opened the National Assembly for Wales at Cardiff, welcoming it as "a bridge into the future". In July of the same year, The Queen opened the Scottish Parliament in Edinburgh, in a day of ceremony and celebration marking, in her own words, "the threshold of a new constitutional age".

As the world grew smaller through new communications technologies, The Queen paid State Visits to places never previously accessible to her, including the former countries of the Eastern Bloc - Hungary (1993), Russia (1994), Poland (1996) and the Czech Republic (1996). History was also made in the reciprocal State Visits of The Queen and President Nelson Mandela of South Africa in 1995 and 1996. The launch of the British Monarchy web-site in 1997 allowed an even larger global audience to learn more about the role and work of The Queen and the Royal Family.

Date	Event	Location
11 Jul	The Queen will visit Leeds Civic Centre	Leeds
11 Jul	The Queen will visit the set of 'Emmerdale'	Leeds
12 Jul	The Queen accompanied by the Duke of Edinburgh will attend a Service for Rural Life	Beverley
12 Jul	The Queen, accompanied by The Duke of Edinburgh, will visit Beverley Racecourse	Beverley
16 Jul	The Queen accompanied by The Duke of Edinburgh, will give a Garden Party	London
17 Jul	The Queen accompanied by The Duke of Edinburgh will attend Lunch at the Athenaeum Restaurant	Bury St. Edmunds
17 Jul	The Queen will visit Ipswich.	Ipswich
17 Jul	The Queen will visit Stowmarket in Suffolk.	Stowmarket
18 Jul	The Queen accompanied by The Duke of Edinburgh will open the Millennium Library in Norwich.	Norwich
18 Jul	The Queen, accompanied by The Duke of Edinburgh, will visit Castle Museum, Norwich.	Norwich
18 Jul	The Queen, and The Duke of Edinburgh, will give a Garden Party at Sandringham House	Sandringham
23 Jul	The Queen will attend a Gala at Covent Garden.	London
23 Jul	The Queen will open the new Greater London Authority Building	London
24 Jul	The Queen will attend a service at Manchester Cathedral.	Manchester
24 Jul	The Queen will visit Christie Hospital in Manchester.	Manchester
24 Jul	The Queen will visit the King's School, Macclesfield.	Macclesfield
25 Jul	The Queen will open the Commonwealth Games in Manchester.	Manchester
25 Jul	The Queen will visit Liverpool Town Hall.	Liverpool

The Queen and Duke of Edinburgh had more grandchildren with the birth of two sons to The Prince and Princess of Wales and two daughters to The Duke and Duchess of York

The decade had its share of sadness, including the fire which caused significant damage at Windsor Castle. The tragic death of Diana, Princess of Wales, caused widespread public mourning in 1997. The Queen broadcast to the nation on the eve of the Princess's funeral, paying tribute to her life and work.

More recently, at the start of her Jubilee year, there was more heartache with the deaths of Princess Margaret and then, of Queen Elizabeth The Queen Mother.

There were also happier times. The restoration of Windsor Castle was testimony to the flourishing of modern craftsmanship. The Queen led the nation in celebrations for the 50th anniversary of the end of the Second World War in Europe, the arrival of the new Millennium, the 100th birthday of Queen Elizabeth The Queen Mother, the wedding of Prince Edward and Sophie Rhys-Jones, and the Golden Wedding anniversary of herself and Prince Philip.

In 2002, The Queen's Golden Jubilee will be celebrated with public events and visits by The Queen and Prince Philip throughout the UK and Commonwealth. Only four earlier monarchs have achieved this milestone. In the course of her fifty-year reign, The Queen has undertaken more official duties and met more of her subjects than any of her predecessors. It is an event worth celebrating!

Date	Event	Location
25 Jul	The Queen will visit Walker Art Gallery in Liverpool.	Liverpool
26 Jul	The Queen will visit Commonwealth Games venues in Greater Manchester.	Manchester
30 Jul	Garden party for representatives of charities of which The Queen is Patron.	London
31 Jul	The Queen will attend a performance at the National Ice Centre in Nottingham.	Nottingham
31 Jul	The Queen will visit Lindsey Lodge Hospice in Scunthorpe.	Scunthorpe
31 Jul	The Queen will visit Normanby Hall and the city centre in Scunthorpe.	Scunthorpe
1 Aug	The Queen accompanied by The Duke of Edinburgh will visit Leicester City Centre.	Leicester
1 Aug	The Queen will visit Leicester City Centre and the National Space Centre.	Leicester
1 Aug	The Queen will visit Pride Park in Derby.	Derby
4 Aug	The Queen will close the Commonwealth Games in Manchester.	Manchester
5 Aug	The Queen accompanied by The Duke of Edinburgh will visit the Edinburgh Tattoo.	Edinburgh
5 Aug	The Queen will attend a community event and a reception in Preston.	Preston
5 Aug	The Queen will attend a garden party at Cumbria Castle.	Carlisle
7 Aug	The Queen accompanied by The Duke of Edinburgh, will give a Garden Party at Balmoral Castle.	Ballater

Who says the good guys never win?

Why should only profit-obsessed plc's make it in the market place? Look at the Co-operative Group, the country's leading consumer co-operative. One of our main concerns is to give our customers the best products at the best value. After all, they do own us. Being committed to openness, honesty and social responsibility hasn't stopped us becoming a highly successful family of businesses. A winning formula, it would seem. For more on the Co-operative Group, call 0800 0686 747 or visit www.co-op.co.uk

the Co-operative Group

Co-operative Group (CWS) Limited,
New Century House, Manchester M60 4ES. Registered Number 525R.

Commonwealth *Affair*

By Ron Allison

A familiar figure, a familiar scene - Her Majesty Queen Elizabeth II in the middle of an enormous crowd, Prince Philip by her side. Whether at the opening ceremony of the Commonwealth Games or on a royal "walkabout", the warmth of the welcome given to the Queen as she visits any one of the fifty-four independent member states of the Commonwealth is invariably the same.

The Queen arrives for the opening ceremony of the 1994 Commonwealth Games in Victoria, Canada.

They might be in Sydney, Australia or Bridgetown, Barbados. The location could be a township in South Africa or the centre of Nairobi in Kenya. They might be in the far north of Canada or on one of the islands of the South Pacific; it really would not make any difference. Even if the political leaders - or at least some of them - are not seeing eye to eye at any given time the Queen herself is respected and greeted on her own behalf. She is accepted for who she is. True she has come from London but she has done so as Head of the Commonwealth.

The Queen would be smiling, no doubt carrying at least one bouquet of flowers. The crowds, young and old, would be responding. The chances are that the weather would be warm, if not hot, the royals would be in town and the town would be "en fete". And no one would be enjoying it more than the Queen herself.

Indeed there can be few people, if any, who care as passionately about the Commonwealth as she does or who work so diligently on its behalf. As with all her responsibilities, the Queen carries out her role as Commonwealth Head with total dedication. She makes certain she always has the time for the duties involved - whether, for example, receiving a newly appointed High Commissioner in Buckingham Palace or touring the islands of the Caribbean.

Traditionally dressed women greet the Queen as she disembarks the Queen's Flight for an official visit to Malawi, Africa in July 1979.

Warmest Wishes from Barbados

The Rt. Hon. Owen S. Arthur
Prime Minister.

50 GOLDEN YEARS

The Government and people of Barbados pay tribute to Your Majesty, Queen Elizabeth II, on the historic occasion of your Golden Jubilee.

The people of Barbados recall many fond memories of your visits to our shores during 1975 and 1989.

We wish to use this opportunity to express our deepest sentiments to you, on this grand occasion.

OWEN S. ARTHUR
Prime Minister.

Her Majesty knights cricketing legend
Sir Garfield Sobers, 1975.

Her Majesty and Governor General
Sir Hugh Springer, 1989.

President of the Senate, Sir Frank Walcott
introduces Speaker of the House of Assembly,
Hon. Lawson Weekes to Her Majesty, 1989.

Her Majesty stops to chat with school children
on her 1989 visit.

Our Thanks To Her Majesty

It is a privilege to have this opportunity to express sincere congratulations to Her Majesty, Queen Elizabeth II on the Golden Jubilee of her reign.

We would also like to use this occasion to extend our appreciation to Her Majesty for her caring commitment, visionary guidance and generous friendship and service to that family of nations, the Commonwealth, of which Barbados is a proud member. The bond of fellowship and cooperation that unites Commonwealth members has been a powerful force in fostering economic development in all our nations. It is very fitting that the Her Majesty's association should be celebrated as, "50 Golden Years", for her contribution has indeed been as precious and rewarding to the recipients as any gifts of that noble metal would be.

Queen Elizabeth is very special to all Barbadians, for Her Majesty has honoured our island with a number of visits including that momentous and joyous occasion in 1975 when she bestowed knighthood on Sir Garfield Sobers, our living National Hero and a continuing inspiration to legions of sports persons and fans around the Commonwealth and across the world.

Thank you, Your Majesty. May you enjoy many more years of good health and happy fulfillment in your duties.

Central Bank Of Barbados

Tom Adams Financial Centre, Spry Street,
Bridgetown, Barbados, West Indies
Tel: (246) 436-6870 **Fax:** (246) 427-9559
E-mail: cbb.libr@caribsurf.com
Web: http://www.centralbank.org.bb/

Princess Margaret greets the Queen and Prince Philip when they arrived for a visit to Mustique during their Jubilee tour in 1977.

About one quarter of the world's population lives in the Commonwealth. Almost all the member countries used to be under British rule but each is now a totally independent state. Some, like Australia and Canada, New Zealand and Jamaica are still monarchies - the Queen is their Head of State. Others - the majority - have, like India in the first instance, chosen to become republics but to remain in the club.

Within that club, incidentally, the United Kingdom is no more than an equal among equals and when the Commonwealth Heads meet in conference the British prime minister has no seniority over any other leader. The changes that bought about this situation during the second half of the twentieth century are a matter of some pride. Speaking in London during her Silver Jubilee celebrations, the Queen said the Commonwealth demonstrated "the transformation of the Crown from an emblem of dominion into a symbol of free and voluntary association. In all history this has no precedence"

It is not too difficult to understand why it all means so much to the Queen. She grew up in the days of the British Empire, when so much of a world map was coloured red, and she saw at first hand during the second world war what that meant in practice. Men and women from literally across the world volunteered in their thousands to fight alongside the United Kingdom. Then in the post-war period and beyond came the transition, not by any means peaceful in every case, from colony to nation and the new arrangements and understandings evolved. Is it any wonder she cares as she does? She knows the Commonwealth for its worth and its value. Her feelings are intensely personal.

"

...the transformation of the Crown from an emblem of dominion into a symbol of free and voluntary association. In all history this has no precedence.

"

Above left
Queen Elizabeth II as Head of the Commonwealth with the Commonwealth Prime Ministers at Buckingham Palace, London, at the time of the Commonwealth Conference in London, 3rd February 1953.
Left to Right: Sir G Huggins (South Africa); Mr Mohammed Alim (Pakistan); Mr Robert Menzies (Australia); Mr Charles Swart (South Africa Minister of Justice representing the Prime Minister); Sir Winston Churchill; Mr Sydney Holland (New Zealand); Mr Louis St Laurent (Canada); Mr Pandit Jawaharlal Nehru (India) and Sir John Kotelawala.

Below left
The Queen poses for a formal group photograph with Heads of Government attending the Commonwealth Conference in Lusaka, Zambia in 1979.

Two regular features of the organisation's life are the bi-annual meetings of the Heads of Government and the four-yearly Commonwealth Games. The former took place in Brisbane, Australia in March while the games will be held in Manchester, England this summer. The Queen attends both and, as she always does at the conferences, arranges private meetings with all the leaders. In many cases this means little more than meeting old acquaintances; in others it's the perfect opportunity to start new friendships. Just as British prime ministers value their weekly meeting with the Queen so too do the presidents and premiers from the Commonwealth. They appreciate the time spent with someone who has "seen it all". A very great deal of wisdom has been accumulated over the years! Other not-to-be missed events are the Commonwealth Day celebrations, including a service at Westminster Abbey, and, of course, the annual message to the Commonwealth, generally known at the Queen's Christmas message.

The Queen opens parliament in Nassau, Bahamas in 1977.

GOVERNMENT OF THE BRITISH VIRGIN ISLANDS

VIGILATE

CHIEF MINISTER
ADMINISTRATION BUILDING
ROAD TOWN, TORTOLA

CONGRATULATIONS

from the British Virgin Islands

The Government and people of the British Virgin Islands salute Your Majesty, Queen Elizabeth II, on the occasion of your Golden Jubilee and 75th Birthday.

Your Majesty is affectionately remembered by the people of the Territory for gracing us with your presence during 1966 and 1977.

Heartfelt congratulations and warmest wishes on this historic occasion!

Ralph T. O'Neal
Chief Minister

photos starting clockwise from top right:

Present day Chief Minister of the Virgin Islands, Hon. Ralph T. O'Neal;

Her Majesty stops to chat with wellwishers in Virgin Gorda on her 1977 visit to the British Virgin Islands;

Her Majesty views locally made crafts, 1977;

Her Majesty and Administrator M. Staveley at West End, Tortola, during her 1966 visit;

Her Majesty tours Tortola on her 1966 visit;

Members of the community welcome Her Majesty, 1977;

The late Chief Minister Hon. Lavity Stoutt accompanies Her Majesty and H.R.H. Prince Philip during her 1977 tour;

Her Majesty with Mr.. Alban Anthony, former member of the Legislative Council, 1977.

So the " great and the good" have their moments but it is when she is out among the "ordinary" people that the Queen is best seen to be about her Commonwealth business. On a walkabout in a town centre, visiting children at school or the sick in hospital, shopping in a street-market, chatting to sheep-shearers in Queensland or eating roast suckling pig at an outdoor feast in Tonga - these are the kind of "engagements" that are such fun. They take on a spontaneous, unplanned life of their own. So many people throughout the Commonwealth seem to know instinctively how to meet and greet the Queen and Prince Philip with great respect yet with uninhibited, infectious good humour. All this strengthens the links and helps to remove even further the legacies of the colonial days and the resentments of the past.

My own involvement with the royal family in the 'sixties and 'seventies took me to many parts of the Commonwealth. Never, either as a correspondent or as a courtier, was I bored or unimpressed. Each day brought its own delights while all demonstrated the affection that flowed back and forth between the Queen and the crowds. In one sense so little in common, in another, so much!

It now seems appropriate that at the moment she became Queen back in 1952, Elizabeth was at the start of a Commonwealth tour. With the Duke of Edinburgh she was in Kenya and although they had to return to London immediately on hearing of the death of her father, George VI, the couple set out on a world tour of the Commonwealth countries the following year, setting the style for the reign.

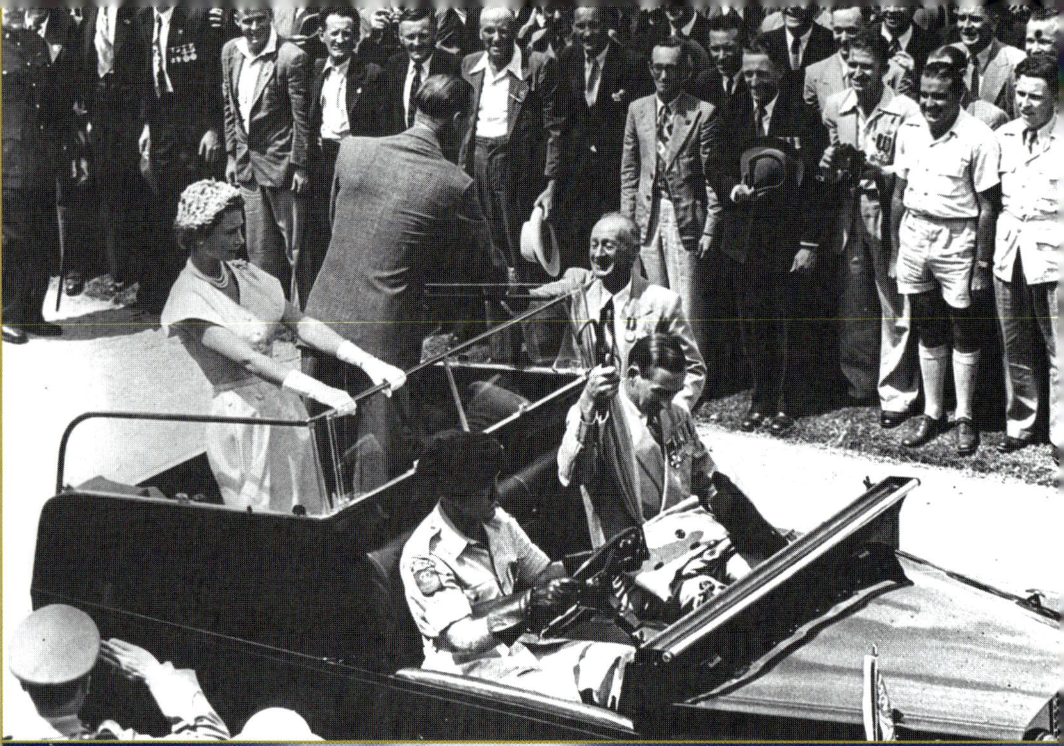

Top
Royal visit to Queensland. At the ex-servicemen and –women rally at Brisbane Oval during the British royal tour of Queensland, 73 year old Navy veteran Bill McLellan steps out of the crowd spontaneously to shake the Duke of Edinburgh's hand. March 1954.

Middle
The Queen visits Belize, October 1985

Bottom
Queen Elizabeth II holds her own umbrella as she rides in an open Rolls Royce between rows of colourfully garbed tribesmen at Kaduna in Northern Nigeria. In the seat with her is her husband, the Duker of Edinburgh, in the uniform of a Field Marshal. Some 6,000 tribesmen put on a spectacular display of dancing, horse riding and acrobatics to please the touring Queen.

THE CHIEF MINISTER 6 CONVENT PLACE GIBRALTAR

On the occasion of the Golden Jubilee of Your Majesty's accession to the throne, it is my honour, on behalf of Your Majesty's loyal government and subjects in Gibraltar, to humbly extend to Your Majesty our gratitude for Her Majesty's reign over Gibraltar during the last 50 years.

In these difficult times for us, I hope that Your Majesty will permit me also to express the desire of Her loyal subjects here that Her Sovereignty, and that of her Successors, will prevail in this part of Her Realm exclusively and indefinitely.

P R Caruana
Chief Minister

Telephone (350) 70071; Fax (350) 76396.

Main Picture
The Queen and King of Tonga at a 'Grand Picnic' held in Her Majesty's honour during her visit to Tonga in 1977.

Inset
The Queen and Prince Philip find local dancers highly amusing during their visit to Tuvalu in 1982.

The Queen gives a speech at a State banquet given for her in Auckland, New Zealand in February 2002.

50 GOLDEN YEARS!

The Government and people of Belize as a proud member of the Commonwealth Community wish Her Majesty Queen Elizabeth II a joyous Golden Jubilee year.

Hon. Said Musa, Prime Minister of Belize

Cape Town

Your Majesty,

On behalf of the municipal council and citizens of Cape Town, it affords me great pleasure to extend to you our warmest congratulations on the occasion of your golden jubilee. South Africa's Mother City recalls with great fondness the visit you and the Duke of Edinburgh paid to Cape Town in 1995, as we do your visit in 1947 during which time you celebrated your 21st birthday.

Between the United Kingdom and South Africa there exists unbreakable bonds bred of friendship, alliance in war, partnership in trade and rivalry on the sporting field. The history of this country and this city is inextricably bound to Great Britain and the far-flung lands that constitute the Commonwealth.

In this joyous year of celebration, we unite with peoples throughout the world to give thanks for your long and dutiful reign and to pray for many more years of good health and benevolent rule. In all nations, but especially the Commonwealth, Your Majesty is held in high regard and great affection, and the City of Cape Town yields to none in its respectful acknowledgement of your jubilee.

Alderman Gerald Morkel

ALDERMAN GERALD MORKEL
MAYOR OF CAPE TOWN

For further information, contact the City Manager on +27 21 400-1335 or e-mail info@capetown.gov.za or Private Bag x9181 Cape Town 8000 or visit the City of Cape Town's website www.capetown.gov.za

CITY OF CAPE TOWN
ISIXEKO ASEKAPA
STAD KAAPSTAD

ST.

Her belief in the concept has been one of the constants in her life - non-negotiable, it might be said . As memorable as any official event in her life was her visit to the South Africa of President Nelson Mandela, some thirty years after she had first gone there as Princess Elizabeth in 1947. It was hugely enjoyed and totally successful. An absolute landmark in the history of the Commonwealth and one of the high points of the reign.

Previous page
The Queen enjoys a walkabout in Moose jaw, Canada in July 1978.

This page
The Queen has an opportunity to meet local people during her visit to Antigua in October 1985.

Next page
Nelson Mandela accompanies The Queen on a walkabout in Cape Town, South Africa in March 1995.

The Queen enjoys a visit to the Hugh Sherlock School in Trenchtown, Jamaica in January 2002. She met many of the pupils, staff and parents.

There have been so many highlights however and many of them have involved the Queen in her position as Head of the Commonwealth. She was not elected as such, nor appointed, it was the wish of the member nations that that is what should happen. How well they have been served!

Message from the Prime Minister of the Commonwealth of The Bahamas

The Golden Jubilee of Her Majesty, Queen Elizabeth II, signifies 50 years of exceptional leadership over a complex group of nations, with diverse cultural, historical, geographical and social circumstances, and united by the strong ties that abound in the Commonwealth of Nations. For over 50 years, this community of nations has witnessed the unswerving commitment by Her Majesty to those principles espoused by the Commonwealth: the promotion and protection of human rights, the advancement of the rights of women, the upholding of democratic ideals and the promotion of justice, tolerance and respect for all people.

Above all, Her Majesty has remained true to the pledge made at the onset of her reign to "...always work as my father did throughout his reign, to uphold constitutional government and to advance the happiness and prosperity of my people, spread as they are the world over." Her Majesty's commitment to this goal earned her the singular accomplishment of making more overseas visits than any other Sovereign prior to her reign and won for her the love of all her people.

The monarchy has evolved during the past 50 years into the modern and accessible one that has been described as a symbol of fraternity. It is as no surprise therefore that Her Majesty wished that the celebration marking her Golden Jubilee reach into every community and involve everyone, no matter their background, age, culture, ethnic origin, religion or other status.

In the Commonwealth of The Bahamas, we recall affectionately the occasions when her Majesty visited our shores. Her warmth and enthusiasm left an indelible impression on all those who had the privilege to encounter her presence.

On the occasion of the Golden Jubilee of Her Majesty Queen Elizabeth II, I am pleased, on behalf of the Government and people of the Commonwealth of The Bahamas, to extend to her heartfelt congratulations, and to thank her for 50 years of outstanding leadership and guidance. We wish upon her and her family God's richest blessings.

Hubert A. Ingraham
Prime Minister, The Commonwealth of The Bahamas

The Queen pictured taking a break ahead of a busy International schedule.

The Commonwealth & Beyond

By Harold Brooks-Baker

The special relationship between Great Britain and the United States is regularly trumpeted on both sides of the Atlantic and never more so than now. The focal point for this important international understanding resides in the figure of the British monarch.

The Queen seen giving a historic speech at the House of Congress in Washington, DC

This strong bond originates not from Elizabeth II but with her parents, George VI and Queen Elizabeth who, at another critical moment in international affairs, visited President Franklin Roosevelt. They stayed with him and his wife Eleanor at the White House in Washington D.C. and at their palatial stately home, Hyde Park, New York.

During World War II, the President and First Lady and the King and Queen worked hard at cementing the trust between their two countries. Orchestrated by Prime Minister Winston Churchill, himself half American, the benefits of this mutual assurance reached into every corner of what was then the British Empire, and later throughout the newly created Commonwealth.

This page
The Queen and Prince Philip seen entertaining President Kennedy and wife Jackie at Buckingham Palace, London in 1961.

Next page
The Queen greets John Kennedy Jnr and Jackie Kennedy. They met at the unveiling of the JFK Memorial in Runnymede, near Windsor in 1965.

GOODWILL MESSAGE BY H.E. THE PRESIDENT, HONOURABLE DANIEL T. ARAP MOI, CGH, MP, ON THE OCCASION OF THE CELEBRATION OF 50 GOLDEN YEARS SINCE HER MAJESTY QUEEN ELIZABETH II'S ACCESSION TO THE THRONE IN 1952.

On this occasion of the celebration of 50 Golden Years since Her Majesty Queen Elizabeth II's Accession to the Throne, I take this opportunity to convey on behalf of the government and the people of Kenya, warm and friendly congratulations to Her Majesty, the government and the people of the United Kingdom.

Kenya and the United Kingdom enjoy warm and fruitful relations dating back to 1963, when Kenya attained her independence. As a member of the Commonwealth, Kenya has continued to maintain strong links with the United Kingdom for the mutual benefit of the two countries.

As the head of the Commonwealth, Her Majesty has been instrumental in creating a true sense of a family amongst all the member countries of the Commonwealth. In this regard, Her Majesty has been the Commonwealth's principal bond, helping to build links amongst the members as well as serving as an inspiration to all members of the club. The Queen has demonstrated in many ways that the Commonwealth occupies a special place in her heart.

In recognition of Her Majesty's unfailing support for the Commonwealth and its programmes, we in Kenya join Her Majesty in celebrating this historic occasion marking 50 Golden Years since her Accession in 1952, and wish her well for the future.

D. ARAP MOI, CGH, MP
PRESIDENT OF THE REPUBLIC OF KENYA

18th December, 2001

MINISTERU
G AS-SERVIZZI EKONOMI I

MALTA

MINISTRY
FOR ECONOMIC SERVICES

Il-Ministru

The Minister

22 March 2002

Majesty,

It is a great honour to extend best wishes on the occasion of Your Majesty's Golden Jubilee.

Over the past years, the United Kingdom and the British Commonwealth have achieved important goals and successfully addressed critical challenges. Your Majesty's strong unifying force and profound sense of duty was instrumental towards this end.

We are today faced with new political and economic realities that underline the need for nations to collaborate further in the pursuit of long-term sustainability. The inter-dependence among nations is indeed a reality, where people of different races and creed must live together in full respect for one another. We must remain faithful to core values and traditions that underpinned our past achievements and which would ensure socio-economic cohesion and equitable development.

Your Majesty's dignity, integrity and strong commitment to service will continue to guide many nations to face the challenges of the future.

JOSEF BONNICI

Her Majesty Queen Elizabeth II
Buckingham Palace
London.

While the lands of the Empire had been painted the traditional Imperial red through colonisation and conquest, the newly independent countries of the Commonwealth more or less chose to be a part of it, and to fulfil their obligations as members.

There are fifty-four member states represented on every continent in both hemispheres. One quarter of the global population is included and so nearly every race, and all religious persuasions, are represented. Despite varying political ideologies, there is a bond, a mutual interest in democracy and the unquestioned learning and teaching of the English language. The Queen is head of state in sixteen of these countries including Canada, Australia and New Zealand and she provides an important link between these countries in the interconnected modern world.

Queen Elizabeth II sits in an open limousine beside President Dwight D. Eisenhower as they await the start of their motorcade into and through Washington D.C. These were less perilous times when personal security for world leaders was less stringent allowing for the public to see their leaders up close and not in closed, armoured limousines as are required in present day situations. October 1957.

Congratulatory Message to Her Majesty, Queen Elizabeth II
During her Golden Jubilee
By the Prime Minister of Papua New Guinea
Hon. Sir Mekere Morauta, Kt MP

On behalf of the Government and the people of Papua New Guinea, I would like to convey sincere felicitations and gratitude to Her Majesty, Queen Elizabeth II on this, the Golden Jubilee, of her reign as Head of the Commonwealth.

Indeed, Her Majesty's 50-year reign has epitomised and embodied the values of stability, integrity and continuity, which I believe will continue in the years ahead.

Her Majesty has witnessed, during her reign - personal tragedy - to public devastation caused by war and natural disasters - to the rebuilding, as well as birth of new nations, into the family of democratic and independent nations in the Commonwealth.

One of these young nations, I am proud to say, is Papua New Guinea which gained Independence in 1975. We had the privilege then to have His Royal Highness, the Prince of Wales, witness this historic occasion, on Her Majesty's behalf.

The people and successive governments of Papua New Guinea have always acknowledged the significance and value of having Her Majesty as our Queen, and head of the Commonwealth.

Her Majesty has visited Papua New Guinea twice. The first was before Independence in 1974 where she was also able to attend the Goroka Show and witness a traditional display of some of the 850 cultures of our country.

These visits are fondly cherished by all in Papua New Guinea as they signify the enduring interest Her Majesty has for us.

We are also proud, as a Member of the Commonwealth, to acknowledge Her Majesty's significant contributions in bringing together the peoples and governments of the Commonwealth of Nations.

Queen Elizabeth II symbolises an enduring sense of belonging, stability and continuity in the association.

The people and Government of Papua New Guinea strongly believe Her Majesty will continue to work together with all leaders of the Commonwealth in building a modern and vibrant association.

We reaffirm the Commonwealth's principles of working to serve our peoples, being an effective defender of democratic freedoms, a peacemaker in conflict, and promoting people-centred economic development.

Papua New Guinea wishes her good health this Golden Jubilee year, and in years to come.

Mekere Morauta
Prime Minister

The Queen's regular visits to every Commonwealth country are an important physical display of the bonds which unite them. She shares this important duty with the Duke of Edinburgh, the Prince of Wales and her daughter and younger sons who carry out official visits on her behalf. When the monarch herself visits one of these sixteen countries (or Realms, as they become during her visit) she is effectively head-of-state and could technically summon parliament. But her role is essentially symbolic.

She acts also as the unifying figure at the Commonwealth Heads of Government meeting held every two years at different locations, this year in Brisbane, Australia. To fully comprehend the workload she bears in this role, a role she carries out with devotion and great diplomatic skill, one has only to look at the countries that make up her Commonwealth.

Maori women greet the Queen during her visit to New Zealand in 1977.

Republic of Nauru

The government and people of the Republic of Nauru extend our warmest and heartfelt congratulations to Her Majesty Queen Elizabeth the second upon the fulfilment of her role as Head of the Commonwealth for the past fifty years.

We thank Her Majesty for her wise and beneficent leadership as Head of the Commonwealth.

We remember with much affection her visit to the shores of the island of Nauru, where we were all inspired by her sense of occasion and calm dignity.

We are indebted for her continued interest and understanding of the problems of the small island states, which form such an integral part of the Commonwealth.

The government and people of the Republic of Nauru extend to Her Majesty their wish for her continued good health and leadership as Head of the Commonwealth.

On behalf of the people of the Republic of Nauru, wishing you ekeatsi, ibibogi me emawir omo ean tsimorum eaeow.

Rene R. Harris

PRESIDENT

The Queen and Prince Philip seen meeting local schoolchildren during their visit to St.Kitt's, Caribbean in 1985.

These are Antigua and Barbuda, Australia, Bangladesh, Barbados, Belize, Botswana, Brunei Darussalam, Cameroon, Canada, Cyprus, Dominica, Fiji Islands, Ghana, Grenada, Guyana, India, Jamaica, Kenya, Kiribati, Lesotho, Malawi, Malaysia, the Maldives, Malta, Mauritius, Mozambique, Namibia, Nauru, New Zealand, Nigeria, Papua New Guinea, Samoa, Seychelles, Sierra Leone, Singapore, the Solomon Islands, South Africa, Sri Lanka, St. Kitts and Nevis, St. Lucia, St. Vincent and the Grenadines, Swaziland, The Bahamas, The Gambia, Tonga, Trinidad and Tobago, Tuvalu, Uganda, the United Kingdom, United Republic of Tanzania, Vanuatu, Zambia and Zimbabwe.

Pakistan should be in this list but, following the military coup in October 1999, the country was suspended.

Many people, especially in the United Kingdom, are ignorant of and appear quite indifferent to the significance of the Commonwealth, particularly in relation to the monarchy. This is not the view of the Queen. She regards this organisation with the same commitment as she does being Sovereign.

The Story of Queen Elizabeth II

Special Golden Jubilee Video for just £14.99

Mention 'The Queen' and the world knows that you are referring to Her Majesty Queen Elizabeth II of Great Britain. 2002 marks the 50th anniversary of Her Majesty's Accession to the throne.

As a celebration of this historic occasion we are delighted to offer our readers the opportunity to buy the Story of Queen Elizabeth II at the special, all inclusive price of £14.99.

In this remarkable double video the BBC's Royal correspondent Jennie Bond tells the life story of Elizabeth Windsor, the longest reining monarch since Queen Victoria.

Using extraordinarily archive footage including rare colour material stretching back to the 1930's, all the most dramatic events in Her Majesty's life are here for you to enjoy. From her marriage to the handsome Prince Philip of Greece, the birth of her son Charles, her glorious coronation to her extravagant tours of the commonwealth and more recently, the 100th birthday of her own indomitable mother, The Queen Mother.

Queen Elizabeth II has witnessed some of the most radical changes in British society in recent history but despite these changes, she remains a noble, respected and much-loved monarch.

Please send me	Qty	Price	Total
Story of Queen Elizabeth II			

I enclose my cheque/PO for £..............................made payable to: **Green Umbrella**

TITLE (Mr/Mrs/Miss/Ms)..............NAME..
(BLOCK CAPITALS)

ADDRESS..

....

....POSTCODE......................................

DAYTIME TEL NUMBER...

OR please debit my credit / debit card with the sum of £...............................

Card No...

Valid From......................Expires......................Issue No (Switch only)......................

Signature ....

To order call our credit card hotline

01371 873138

Alternatively, post the completed coupon opposite together with a cheque/PO to:
QE II Video Offer, PO Box 2616, Great Dunmow, Essex CM6 1DH

PLEASE DO NOT SEND CASH. Offer subject to availability. Allow up to 28 days for delivery from receipt of order. We deliver to addressees within UK (including Northern Ireland).

VHS Running time: 2 x 52 minutes

Previous page
Inset. The Queen inspects a guard of honor in Tiananmen Square, China in 1986.
Main picture. A solemn escort for the Queen as she laid a wreath at the 'Tomb of the Unknown Soldier' in Moscow, Russia in 1994.

This page
The Queen seen taking a military salute on her arrival in Riyadh, Saudi Arabia in 1979. This was the first visit of a British monarch to country.

So where does it fit into the European monarchical tradition? The British monarchy is part of that tradition through close kinship. The answer is that without the Commonwealth the United Kingdom would probably be a minor monarchy, more in a league with Denmark of Holland. Thanks to the Queen's unique presence in this global institution and the enormous experience that longevity has granted her, let alone the strong approval rating of the United States, the Great remains in Great Britain.

It is necessary for Commonwealth countries to fulfil the high standards expected of them and if these are not adhered to nations may be dropped after a thorough investigation by all member states. This not only happend in the case of Pakistan but also with Fiji in 1987 when, following a military coup, the government was removed from office by the Governor-General who took temporary control. A second coup took place in September when Fiji was declared a republic and membership of the Commonwealth lapsed. This state of affairs lasted for 10 years until 1997.

A few years earlier South Africa was famously excluded from this exclusive club because of its support of apartheid. Another "problem" surrounds the former Southern Rhodesia, now known as Zimbabwe, and the question of the expulsion of the white settlers. This unhappy state of affairs illustrates the difficult position in which Elizabeth II can find herself. Even though she, as sovereign, has been designated head of the Commonwealth, it is, in many people's eyes, a purely symbolic position. However, the Queen has the respect of all members, is a wise counsellor to them all, showing neither fear nor favour, and continually handles difficult situations with dexterity.

So far, she has regularly been able to please. Of course all of these countries, with the exception of Mozambique, were either once ruled by the British or directly connected to a Commonwealth country. At the Edinburgh summit conference of 1997, it was agreed that to become a member of the Commonwealth, a country must have had "a constitutional association with an existing Commonwealth member state." It was also made clear that any such country "should also comply with Commonwealth values, principles and priorities, as set out in the Harare (Salisbury, Southern Rhodesia) Declaration and it should accept Commonwealth conventions".

The political values of this great organisation are particularly respected with regard to human rights, the rule of law and sustainable economic and social development.

It still has great prestige. When the Queen or one of her family (acting on her behalf) presents a declaration or a title, the whole world takes notice. After the catastrophe of September 11, the Queen and number 10 Downing Street sent HRH the Duke of York to New York City to present Mr Rudolf Guiliani with an honorary Knighthood.

Honorary Knighthoods have also been given to many other distinguished Americans including, to name but a few, Alistair Cooke (he was born in the United Kingdom), former President George Bush, General Norman Schwarzkopf, and former Secretary of Defence, Casper Weinberger.

The special relationship between the United States and Great Britain continues to strengthen since George VI and Queen Elizabeth (now the Queen Mother) brought the world closer together, with the help of President Roosevelt, before the second world war.

In July last year, President George W. Bush attended an important function at Buckingham Palace, which set the stage for future interaction between the two governments. As Head of State in Great Britain, so much of the Queen's cachet is derived from The Commonwealth

inset
The Queen and President Bill Clinton attend a dinner in Portsmouth to commemorate D-Day. May 1984.

Main Picture
The Queen and Prince Philip seen with President George Bush Jnr and his wife Laura during a visit to Buckingham Palace in 2001.

THE PRIME MINISTER

HONIARA
SOLOMON ISLANDS

MESSAGE OF CONGRATULATIONS

The Government and People of the Solomon Islands extend our warmest and heartfelt congratulations to Her Majesty Queen Elizabeth II on her Golden Jubilee celebration as Queen and Head of the Commonwealth.

Her Majesty's distinguished contribution towards the promotion of peace and unity amongst the people of the Commonwealth of Nations, including our nation, the Solomon Islands, shall be long remembered with respect and affection. The courage and affection Her Majesty has shown irrespective of race, creed or belief is an immense inspiration to us all.

The Government and People of the Solomon Islands are indebted to her Majesty for her understanding of the problems of small island states such as ours. We have always admired her affection and the warmth she has shown on her visits to these islands have been greatly appreciated.

On behalf of the Government and People of the Solomon Islands, I extend to Her Majesty God's blessings and prosperous years ahead.

Hon. Sir Allan Kemakeza

PRIME MINISTER

12th April 2002

P O BOX G J *Telephone: (677) 22202* *Facsimile: (677) 25470*

Leading Light

By James Whitaker

The Queen's education followed a path that excluded her from the social life and conventional knowledge acquired at school – something she later regretted. She has, nevertheless, repeatedly displayed the kind of wisdom only gained through experience.

Her grandson Peter Philips gives the Queen a guided tour of a classroom during a visit to Port Regis School, Dorset in 1991. Peter was a pupil at the school.

The formidable Queen Mary seems to have been the only senior royal who was worried about how well her grand-daughters, Elizabeth and Margaret, were being equipped to face a changing world. She complained to her daughter in law (then the Duchess of York, later to be the Queen Mother) that the children's education should not be confined to a governess.

"I don't know what she meant" commented the Duchess. " I and my sisters only had governesses and we all married well - one of us VERY well."

King George V had no such worries. His only stipulation was that his granddaughters should have good handwriting. He told nannie Marion Crawford (Crawfie), "Teach Margaret and Lilibet to write a decent hand. None of my children could write properly."

The two were of course better educated than this. Under the eagle eye of Queen Mary, Crawfie carefully watched as they were taught singing, dancing, music and drawing. Additionally, the Queen insisted they learned subjects she considered essential for royal children.

So they were tutored in genealogy and the physical geography of the Dominions and India as well as the Empire. With even more foresite, French was added to the curriculum, taught by Mrs Montaudon-Smith, known as Monty. Subsequently, Lilibet and Margaret learned this language at the knee of Antoinette de Bellaigue, a Belgian aristocrat. With her expertise, the two princesses became fluent.

Far Left
Princess Elizabeth takes a ride in an open carriage with her grandmother Queen Mary. London 1938.

Above
King George V1 reads royal papers while his daughter Princess Elizabeth looks over his shoulder. Windsor 1942

Below
Princess Elizabeth makes her first broadcast, accompanied by her younger sister Princess Margaret Rose

For reading matter, the Children's Newspaper was subscribed to - and Punch magazine - while books were limited to the "classics" by Robert Louis Stevenson, Jane Austen and Kipling.

Finally, the old Queen herself took on the duty of taking her granddaughters on cultural expeditions each Monday to such places as the Tower of London and the Royal Mint.

In between, the young Elizabeth (preparing for her destiny) started lessons, on her 13th birthday, on constitutional history. Her tutor was the vice-provost of Eton, Sir Henry Marten. He was not only knowledgeable, he entertained the young princess by keeping a pet raven that would affectionately peck him on his ear.

So while Princess Margaret, until the day she died, would angrily protest at dinner parties in front of her mother about her lack of proper education, Elizabeth was reasonably well catered for.

Although the Queen has never been regarded as a great collector of art, of old books or other relics of academia she was, naturally, a believer in achieving the best possible education for her children and, now, her grandchildren.

It was Prince Philip who led the way on their sons and daughter being educated in "normal" schools with other children. But the Queen was quick to concur.

Apart from official visits to various seats of learning throughout the U.K. and the Commonwealth, the Queen makes her own contribution to the academic world via The Queen's Scholastic Awards. Each year she gives prizes or medals to outstanding students at certain schools or colleges.

Medals are made of silver gilt and are called "The Queen's Medal." These are:-

Britannia Royal Naval College, Dartmouth.

A sword is awarded annually to the Acting Sub-Lieutenant of either the Seaman or Supply specialisations who obtains the best results in leadership and work. Also, six telescopes are awarded to cadets who have completed one year, again in leadership and work. There's a medal for the Acting Sub-Lieutenant who obtains the best results in exams during the third and fourth year's training.

Another sword goes each year to the top officer of the Engineering specialisation at the R.N. Engineering College, Manaton on completion of their three year degree or diploma. Officers who graduate in this subject at Cambridge are also eligible.

Eton College

A sum of money is given for Her Majesty's prizes for French and German. This was set up way before the Princes William and Harry enrolled in this ancient school.

Pangbourne College

A medal goes to the cadet showing the qualities likely to make the finest sailor.

There are similar medals for cadets at the Royal Military College of Australia , RAF College, Cranwell, the Royal Australian Air Force Academy, the Royal Australian Naval College and the Royal Military Academy, Sandhurst. If a cadet wins both the Queen's Medal and the college's Sword of Honour they also get a message of congratulations from HM.

Left
Prince William dressed in the famous Eton uniform.

Middle
The Princess of Wales takes her two sons to school. They were both pupils at Wetherby School, London.1989.

Inset
Prince William's first day at Eton College in September 1995. He is accompanied by his parents, brother and house master.

Touring Milton Keynes Polytechnic in March 1992.

At Rugby School the Queen awards a medal for the best English essay on a historical subject. At Wellington College a medal is given for good conduct while at Winchester College a medal is awarded to the best student in each of English verse, English speech, Latin prose and Latin speech. At St George's Middle School, Dersingham (next to Sandringham) the Queen's Bible is presented for proficiency in religious instruction. Another local award is presented at the King Edward VII school, King's Lynn. A medal goes to the leading scholar.

There are also annual awards for outstanding contributions in the fields of architecture, exploration, poetry, police work and science. The medals, made by the Royal Mint, are the personal gift of the Queen and paid for by her.

Architecture: A Queen's Medal is awarded annually by RIBA for the promotion of architecture. Distinguished past winners have included Charles-Edouard Jeanneret (Le Corbusier), 1953; Dr Nikolaus Pevsner, 1967; Dr R Buckminster Fuller, 1968; Sir Dennis Lasdun, 1977, Charles and Ray Eames, 1979; Sir Norman Foster, 1983 and Lord "Richard" Rodgers, 1985. Exploration: Two Queen's medals are awarded each year by the Royal Geographical Society for achievements in exploration and research. The Founder's medal, instituted by William IV, bears the King's effigy. The Patron's Medal bears the effigy of Queen Victoria. Distinguished winners include Sir John Hunt, 1954; Sir Edmund Hillary, 1958; Captain Jacques Cousteau, 1963; Sir Peter Scott, 1983; Sir Ranulph Fiennes, 1984 and Sir David Attenborough, 1985.

Poetry: Instituted in 1933 by George V, the Queen's Medal for poetry was the idea of the then Poet Laureate John Masefield. Recommendations are made by a committee chaired by the Poet Laureate. The obverse of the medal bears the crowned effigy of the Sovereign; the reverse depicts "Truth emerging from her well, holding the divine flame of inspiration." Past distinguished winners include W.H.Auden, 1936; John Betjeman, 1960; Christopher Fry, 1961; Philip Larkin, 1965; Robert Graves, 1968; Stepher Spender, 1971; Ted Hughes, 1974.

Police Essay: An annual competition is held for the best essay written on professional police subjects. Any serving member of the police force in the United Kingdom or any other Commonwealth country may enter.

BRIGHT FUTURES
THE LONDON INSTITUTE
At the forefront of art, design and communication
The London Institute is made up of five distinguished art and design Colleges:
Camberwell College of Arts
Central Saint Martins College of Art and Design
Chelsea College of Art and Design
London College of Fashion
London College of Printing
Together they make the London Institute a world leader in creativity.
The London Institute is honoured to have received the Queen's Anniversary Prize twice; in 1996 for pioneering work in the conservation of works of art on paper at Camberwell, and again in 1998 for creativity and innovation in fashion education at Central Saint Martins.
For further information contact:
Communications & Marketing Office
The London Institute
65 Davies Street, London W1K 5DA
T 020 7514 6130 F 020 7514 6131
E marcom@linst.ac.uk www.linst.ac.uk
The Queen's Anniversary Prizes 1998
ANNA-NICOLE ZIESCHE, MA FASHION

Science: Three Queen's Medals are awarded annually by the Royal Society for outstanding contributions to the sciences in the Commonwealth. Two are awarded in the field of natural science; the third is for applied science and was instituted by the Queen in 1965. Distinguished past winners include Professor Alfred Lovell,1960; Christopher Cockerell, 1966; Dr Max Perutz, 1971; Sir Martin Ryle, 1973; Sir Fred Hoyle, 1974 and Sir Barnes Wallis, 1975.

In addition to her involvement in all the above schools and academies of learning, the Queen is a Patron or Visitor to 81 schools, colleges and Universities.

One of her favourite awards is the Queen's Prize which is handed out annually to the most outstanding student in the Department of English at Bonn University. Instituted in 1965 at the personal wish of the Queen to mark her State Visit to Germany that year, the prize continues a long association between the British Royal Family and the University of Bonn, dating from the 1830s when Prince Albert was a student there.

The winning student receives British books and is given a study visit of about ten days to the United Kingdom, paid for by the British Council. The council arranges for the student to meet authors or academics in his or her field of study and to visit exhibitions and artistic performances.

In the same year, to commemorate Her Majesty's visit to Berlin, the Queen's Lecture was started. Extraordinarily gifted lecturers spoke over the years at the University. Sir Mortimer Wheeler, Sir Kenneth Clarke, Sir Bernard Lovell, Sir Anthony Blunt, Sir Peter Hall and Sir Michael Swan were just a few to address students.

They were halted in 1975 when the British Ambassador in Germany recommended that the lectures in their present form should cease as they were attracting "smaller and less important audiences."

It was suggested - and approved by the Queen - that in future they should be replaced by an annual lecture in Berlin, arranged by the British Council.

The Queen seen during her tour of the Port Regis School in Dorset in 1991. The Queen's two grandchildren Peter and Zara Philips both attended the school.

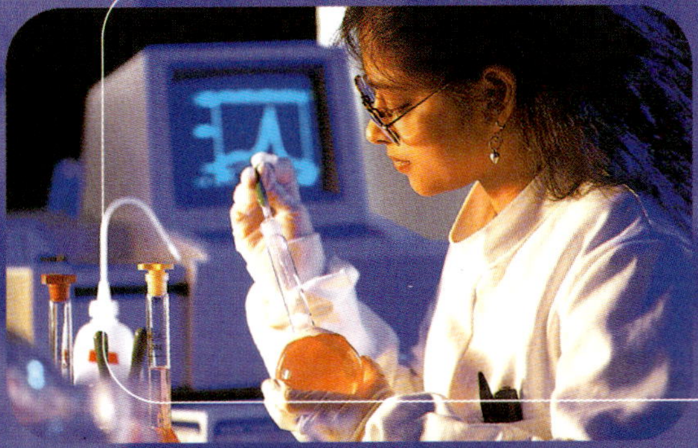

Sporting *Glory*

By Robert Hardman

It is probably just as well that The Queen is not an avid fan of the major sports. For, if she was, who on earth would she support? Quite apart from the thorny issue of which club or county to follow, she would find it hard to choose a nation.

The Queen presents an FA Cup Medal to Stanley Matthews after Blackpool beat Bolton Wanderers 4 – 3. May 1953.

British jockey Sir Gordon Richards (1904 – 1986) riding the joint favourite 'Pinza', wins his first Derby in June 1953. It was his 28th attempt and was a double triumph coming soon after receiving his knighthood.

For whom do you cheer when you are the head of state for no less than 18 international football teams, seven first class international rugby squads and four cricketing Test sides? No wonder she prefers the more individualistic pursuit of racing.

But she is well aware of the place and the role of sport in the lives of all her nations. That is why, looking back over her reign, we see that she has been at the forefront of a remarkable range of events - even if they were hardly her own cup of tea.

Indeed, her reign began with two sporting triumphs which are still remembered fondly to this day. To football fans, the 1953 FA Cup Final will always be remembered as the Stanley Matthews final when the ageing hero (38 is certainly ageing in footballing terms) took his Blackpool side to Wembley and led them to one of the most exciting victories in history.

From 3-1 down against Bolton Wanderers, Matthews and his men went on to win 4-3.

And it was the Queen, attending her first ever soccer match, who presented the great trophy to the great man.

With the Coronation just weeks away, the occasion seemed to encapsulate the new mood of confidence breaking through the gloom of post-war austerity. Indeed, for many British sports fans, the new monarch seemed to be a lucky talisman.

England managed to regain cricket's holy grail, The Ashes, from Australia in that glorious, Everest-conquering Coronation summer. Meanwhile, one suspects that the most exciting sporting moment for the Queen herself was the one which took place at Epsom. Gordon Richards, that titan of the turf, had won every conceivable race with the glaring exception of the Derby.

In fact, he had failed to win it 27 times. It was in 1953, in front of the new monarch and 100,000 of her near-hysterical subjects, that he finally clinched the great prize.

1952 - 2002

In 1952, the year of Her Majesty Queen Elizabeth II's accession to the throne, the Directors, staff and fans of Newcastle United Football Club proudly sang "God Save the Queen" at Wembley Stadium before being crowned FA Cup Winners after a 1-0 victory over Arsenal.

NEWCASTLE UNITED

50 years on, The Directors, staff and fans of Newcastle United Football Club once again take great pride in joining together to congratulate Her Majesty on the occasion of her Golden Jubilee.

Inevitably, this fairytale sequence of sporting events could not last indefinitely but the Queen has always given her support to this vital strand of any nation's life through the ups and downs.

She may not be especially passionate about some sports but she has always appreciated that sport matters greatly to others which means that it is her duty to support it. After all, she is not particularly interested in heavy industry but she has still launched plenty of ships and opened countless factories.

Most of her sporting encounters have, in fact, been at the grass roots level. For every Cup Final she has attended she has sat through a thousand displays on school playgrounds from Perth, Scotland to Perth, Australia.

I have seen her watching everything from judo in New Zealand to junior cricket in Soweto and she has always managed to maintain a healthy interest when lesser eyelids would have come crashing down.

Inevitably, though, it is the major occasions with which she is usually associated. She was there in the royal box at Wembley Stadium to witness the greatest footballing moment in British history, the 1966 World Cup Final.

It did not matter that she would have been pushed to name half of the team who beat Germany that day. The fact that a British monarch was on hand to present the World Cup to a victorious England captain on home soil was the crowning moment to a day of intense national pride.

1966 World Cup –
Bobby Moore accepts the trophy

With the smooth, of course, comes the rough. Thirty years later, she was in the same stadium to present the 1996 European Championship trophy to the Germans, fresh from their semi-final victory over England. When there has been a major global sporting event on British soil - such as the World Cups of rugby and cricket as well as football - she has been there to give it the seal of royal approval.

Indeed, the 1999 Rugby Union World Cup final provided another of those immortal royal sporting moments. The game took place on the very weekend that the Australian public were voting on whether to retain the Queen as their head of state. No sooner had the Queen won the vote than Australia won the World Cup and the former handed the latter the trophy in the royal box at Twickenham. Hollywood could not have scripted it better.

Smiling victors Sherpa Tensing (left) and Edmund Hillary at their camp after their return from Everest.

Rugby union, incidentally, remains the most popular ball game for members of the Royal Family. The Duke of York and the Earl of Wessex both played it during their Gordonstoun schooldays and beyond - the Duke at Lakefield College in Canada and the Earl at Cambridge University.

The Princess Royal remains a devoted patron of the Scottish Rugby Football Union while her son, Peter Phillips, became the first royal rugby international when he turned out for Scotland's schoolboys.

The Queen has always been there for her other nations when putting on the big events. When Montreal staged the 1976 Olympics, the Queen of Canada did the honours. She has been an assiduous attender of Commonwealth Games over the years and will be the focal point of this year's gathering in Manchester at both the opening (July 25) and closing (August 4) ceremonies.

When it was Sydney's turn to hold the 2000 Games, however, the Australians made it clear that they would prefer a native Australian to open the greatest show in the nation's history. Some regarded this as a serious snub to the Queen. Not so the monarch herself. She flew out to Australia a few months before the Games and opened the Olympic Stadium instead.

Inevitably, being British-based means that she attends more sporting events in the United Kingdom than elsewhere. But when touring sides from realms or Commonwealth nations arrive in Britain, there is often an invitation to a Palace reception in their honour. During the 1998 Football World Cup across the Channel in France, the Queen, once again, found her loyalties pulled in three directions. Should she support England, Jamaica or Scotland? In the event, she turned the question on its head and invited the players from all three squads round to Buckingham Palace when it was all over.

John Eales, the Australian captain receives the Rugby World Cup from the Queen in 1999. Australia beat France at the Millennium stadium in Cardiff, Wales.

The Queen watches as the champion, Virginia Wade, shows the trophy to the crowd on the Centre Court at Wimbledon following her victory in the final over the Dutch girl Betty Stove.

There are, however, some sports which she clearly prefers to avoid. It is no secret that the Queen has little time for one of the Duke of Edinburgh's favourite pursuits - yachting. In the early years of her reign, she put in the odd appearance at the annual Cowes Week regatta on the Isle of Wight, Britain's major annual yachting event, but her interest soon paled. Year after year, both the Duke and the Royal Yacht would be there. But, year after year, the Queen failed to appear.

Some have put it down to the weather, others to the fact that yachting is a very dull spectator sport for those who do not sail. A third explanation, offered by one courtier, is that on her last visit, she was the victim of a practical joke. It is said that the Duke's old sailing chum, the boisterous Uffa Fox, had thought that it would be rather amusing to place a "Whoopee" cushion under the royal armchair after a Britannia dinner. The Queen is said to have been so unamused that she never returned.

Another national sporting institution which has also failed to capture the regal imagination is the annual tennis championship at Wimbledon. Other members of the Royal Family have grown to love this event but, for some reason, it has never grabbed the Queen. And yet, on her only visit to the event, Britain was blessed with another touch of that Coronation-style magic.

The year was 1977, the Queen's Silver Jubilee, and the match in question was the Ladies' Final. The victor was Britain's Virginia Wade and no Briton has won a singles title since. Is it too much to hope that in this, her Golden Jubilee year, the Queen returns to those famous grass courts once more to give the home nation its first triumph in 25 years?

SCOTTISH
RUGBY UNION

The Scottish Rugby Union extends loyal greetings to Her Majesty The Queen as the nation and commonwealth celebrate the 50th anniversary of her ascension to the throne.

All in Scottish rugby recall fondly Her Majesty's visit to Murrayfield Stadium in February 1976 - a visit that co-incided with a 22-12 Calcutta Cup victory for Scotland against England.

The links between the Royal Family and Scottish rugby are strong. Indeed, the Queen's grandson, Peter Phillips, has represented Scottish Schools as a back-row forward. We are particularly indebted, too, to the indefatigable support we receive from our Patron, Her Royal Highness The Princess Royal.

Graham Young

President

Scottish Rugby Union

The Derby race, Epsom 1991.The Queen and Queen Mother get excited as the horses approach the finish line.

Pursuits
& PASSIONS

By Richard Kay

Emotion is the one thing the Queen is not allowed to show. Monarchs are above such earthly weakness. Sometimes, however, the pressure is just too much and those immovable features are fractured by a burst of excitement which, on occasion, has even been accompanied by Her Majesty punching the air.

Such moments are inevitably confined to the racetrack where the passions of the Queen are finely focused, even though, as she would admit herself, her failure to win a classic race since her Silver Jubilee 25 years ago hardly makes her the Queen of the track.

The Queen loves horses. They are her main interest and have been her companions since the moment, as a toddler, she was first placed astride one. Even at 76, she rides at Windsor, Balmoral and at Sandringham; always wearing a headscarf but, to the consternation of her advisors, never wearing a hard hat. A risky approach to a potentially dangerous pastime, but so far as we know, she has never come off.

At the track she loves the thrill of the race, but even when her horse is odds-on to win, she never bets. The handbag placed so carefully across her right forearm contains no cash, anyway, except for one race-day a year when a £5 note is carefully placed inside it by her dresser Angela Kelly.

This is Derby Day when the Queen allows herself to be so carried away by the excitement of the Epsom Downs classic - the closest she has come to winning it was when her horse Aureole was second in Coronation Year 1953 - that she participates in a royal family sweepstake. The fivers are piled into a silver rose bowl and it's "winner take all." The best judge of horseflesh in the family, and that included the Queen Mother, the Queen wins this sweepstake regularly.

Queen Elizabeth II on horseback with her two children Princess Anne and Prince Charles in 1956.

Inset
The Queen enjoys a ride in the hills overlooking her Balmoral estate, Scotland.

She loves being with horses, watching them train and often goes to the Royal Stud at Sandringham to be on hand at the stallion station when her mares are being covered. So just how would the Queen relax without horses and racing? Well, she does have other hobbies, such as racing pigeons, budgerigars and, of course, her corgi dogs.

The pigeons are bred at Sandringham - a tradition begun by the Queen's great grandparents King Edward VII and Queen Alexandra - and raced from a loft in King's Lynn, Norfolk. She seldom sees her pigeons, unlike the budgerigars - jokingly known as 'the Queen's flight' - which are bred at Windsor whose noisy aviary she often visits.

Right
Princess Elizabeth at Balmoral Castle with one of her corgis in September 1952.

Inset
Princess Elizabeth aged 10 with two corgis in the garden of 145 Piccadilly.

There are 100 birds, looked after by keeper Graham Stone, all bred from a single pair given to the young Elizabeth during the 1930s.

As for the corgis, the Queen's affection for these spirited little dogs is as great as her love of horses. When she travels between Buckingham Palace and Windsor Castle there is always a self-important, primped-up Corgi lounging on a sheepskin rug on the parcel shelf inside the back window of the royal limousine. In her homes they are always around her feet. She feeds them herself, spooning out the dogfood - specially prepared, not out of cans - into silver bowls.

And when she takes them for a walk, she likes to indulge her other passion, her flower garden. We tend to think only of the Prince of Wales when we think of gardens and the royal family, but Charles clearly gets his love of flowers from his mother.

Just like her eldest son, the Queen is always personally involved when new flowerbeds are being arranged and planted at Buckingham Palace. She is full of ideas, all of which are always discussed with her head gardener, Mark Lane, on site.She takes the same care and control of her flowerbeds at Frogmore, the royal burial area in Windsor Great Park where she walks the dogs at weekends. She especially adores roses, and their scent.

Casually dressed and accompanied by a gun dog. The Queen seen at a pheasant shoot on her Sandringham estate, Norfolk in 1982.

ELIZABETH·II·D·G·REG·F·D·2002
IRB

As a teenager the Queen hunted regularly with the Pytchley in Leicestershire. She was a hard-riding Princess who often troubled her father King George VI with the way she hurled her mount over hedges and ditches. But as a young woman, and certainly by the time she became Queen, she stopped riding to hounds, just as she stopped stalking.

It seems that these blood sports were not in tune with monarchy, though they are keenly followed and supported by most of her family.

The Queen did not entirely desert these country pursuits, however, and even now when the guns are blazing at pheasants at Sandringham or grouse at Balmoral you are likely to find her quiet presence, in a headscarf, following the guns and appreciating the expertise of the best shots.

But wherever she is, and especially now that she has a mobile telephone, she ensures she is never out of touch with her horses and the people who train them.

Until his death last year (2001) her racing manager Lord Carnarvon could safely make the claim that a day did not pass when they did not talk of the sport of kings and queens.

At 76, the Queen has one unfulfilled racing dream....how she would love to own a Derby winner in this her Golden Jubilee year.

Above
The Queen is a keen breeder of racing pigeons. They are bred at her Sandringham estate and raced from King's Lyn, Norfolk.

Right
The Queen shows her love of dogs during a walk on her Balmoral estate.

BY RICHARD KAY

By now, and certainly in any other country, they would have faded into little more than an amusing memory; something for the current crop of schoolchildren to smile about when they opened their history books in search of the lighter moments of past centuries.

The Queen greets guests attending a Buckingham Palace garden party in July 2001.

GARDEN *Parties*

But the Queen's garden parties at Buckingham Palace are still with us. Indeed, they are bigger then ever, serve more cups of English tea (in fact it's a special Darjeeling blend), dainty sandwiches with their crusts removed, and exquisite little cakes than ever before.

On offer is iced coffee, ice cream and something called 'Lemon Refresher' - a fruit squash. But no alcohol.

"Prince Albert... saw them as a sensible and pleasant way of informally meeting a broad cross section of society"

Two bands play, both military and never at the same time. When one finishes its programme, a flag is raised to signal discreetly to the other, across the lawn, that it is their turn. Quaint.

Each summer the Queen holds four garden parties, three of them in her private 40-acre walled garden behind Buckingham Palace while another takes place at the Palace of Holyroodhouse in Edinburgh.

Around 8,000 people go to each, a mix of diplomats, politicians, the armed services, local councillors, charity workers...every sort of contributor to public life.

They were started in 1860 by Queen Victoria, probably at the suggestion of her modernising German husband Prince Albert, who saw them as a sensible and pleasant way of informally meeting a broad cross section of society and, in particular, people whom the Queen would not normally meet. Sadly, he never lived to see them take root in the summer calendar of royal life, as he died in 1861.

People from all walks of life continue to make up the invitation list, although you have to wait to receive one. You cannot apply for tickets. But does the Queen, with other senior members of her family who accompany her, actually meet many?

Sadly, the answer is No. As the fan of 'lines', as they are officially called, open up to be "worked" by each member of the royal family, selected people will have been warned in advance by the Queen's Gentlemen Ushers that they will be spoken to.

Guests who meet the royal family over tea in a special tent, separated from the rest, have to be either in the government or in the diplomatic corps, or a VIP such as the Archbishop of Canterbury.

Nowadays, few people come alone to these delightful two-hour garden parties (in July) that begin on the stroke of 4, when the Queen emerges to walk down the palace steps, pausing for the national anthem to be played, and end at 6 p.m. precisely.

Guests at the first garden party of the season seen in the crowd near Yeomen warders. Buckingham Palace, July 1999.

The scene of a summer garden party at Buckingham Palace, London. Guests stroll about the lawns by the lake and crowd in to the tea tents.

Acknowledging the changing pattern of domestic life, partners are now as welcome as husbands or wives. Until 1993, those invited were permitted only to bring their spouse or an unmarried daughter between the ages of 18 and 25 - a throwback to the abandoned days of debutantes and presentations at court.

Another change involves what to wear. Morning dress or uniform, or even national dress, used to be obligatory. But now softening attitudes has made the choice optional. Few women, however, do not wear a hat.

These parties are a uniquely British way for our Head of State to say thank you to ordinary people who have made a contribution to the life and welfare of the nation. They may not get to meet Her Majesty, but they will always have the invitation to keep on their mantlepiece.

Opposite
The Queen and Prince Philip seen amongst the crowd at a garden party.

Inset top
Crowded tea tents

2nd down
Queen and Duke arrive for the garden party.

3rd down
Some of the lucky guests find a seat on the busy lawns at Buckingham Palace

4th down
The Queen and Duke arrive for a garden party at Holyrood Palace, Scotland 2001.

The Queen's *Good Taste*

By Iwona Whitaker

The Queen likes simple food, keeps to a routine, is a great believer in the regime advocated by Weight Watchers and virtually never takes pills. As a result. she is in good health and keeps her weight under nine stone, perfect for her height of 5ft 4 inches.

The Queen pictured during a visit to Castlemilk Green near Glasgow, Scotland in 1999. She was invited for afternoon tea by Mrs Susan McCarren.

When Bobo (Margaret McDonald), her faithful servant of 60 years died in September 1993 the Queen was devastated. Her Majesty had no greater confidante. They slept together in the nursery when Lilibet was a baby.

Nanny's habits, instilled into this child and through most of her adulthood as Queen, are her guiding light to this day.

At 7.30am a cup of tea is served by a maid who also takes to her newspapers and private mail. The only time this routine was changed was on Bobo's birthday when Her Majesty would take tea to HER.

After dressing, the Queen has breakfast at 8.30 am in a small dining room, close to her bedroom on the first floor of Buckingham Palace. She again has tea and enjoys toast and marmalade. Occasionally, she will have a poached or boiled egg. Maybe, even a piece of bacon.

Prince Philip, unless he has a particularly early start, joins the Queen for breakfast. He prefers to drink coffee. If the Duke is away, the Queen will busy herself doing the Daily Telegraph crossword before making her daily telephone calls to the Queen Mother and Princess Margaret.

If time permits, she will walk her corgis in the Palace grounds although one of her footmen will have also done this first thing.

Top
Some of The Queen's luggage during one of her overseas tours. Clearly visible are the bottles of Malvern water she takes everywhere.

Center inset
Fresh organic vegetables from the royal estates are carried aboard the Royal Yacht Britannia.

Small inset bottom
A pint of unpasteurised milk from the royal farms bottled in The Queen's own bottles.

Lunch is served at 1.10 pm and is always light unless there is an official reception for a visiting VIP or even Head of State.

The Queen and Prince Philip will share a cold buffet of meats and salads, followed by cheese and biscuits. Throughout, the Queen will drink Malvern water (bottles and bottles of this stuff go on overseas tours with her) or maybe orange squash. Prince Philip enjoys a glass of beer.

At an official lunch which will last one and three quarter hours including speeches, the Queen chooses not to sit at the head of the immaculately polished table but somewhere in the middle with Prince Philip often facing her.

There is a real ritual about these occasions. During the first and second courses the Queen talks to the person on her right and when the pudding and cheese are served she talks to the guest on her left. If possible, she tries to have at least a few words with everybody invited.

One of the Queen's favourite dishes at lunch is called "Egg Drum Kilbo" - a mixture of chopped egg and lobster served in a small cocotte dish.

The main course might be Escalope of veal, lamb cutlets, poached salmon or sole meuniere (with grapes). There are always plenty of vegetables (all trimmed and cut to the exact same size) while salad is served on a separate plate together with the main course.

Pudding is often apple tart, lemon mousse or a pavlova with kiwi fruit.

The Queen likes, whenever possible, to get all fresh ingredients from one of the royal farms with wild salmon coming down from Scotland, game from Sandringham and milk, cream and vegetables from Windsor. Naturally, they will be in the peak of condition and served in season.

In the evening the Queen and Prince Philip enjoy a T.V. dinner. The food is served in the Queen's dining room, with the door wide open into the sitting room which has the biggest size T.V. possible.

The Queen enjoys a dry martini and the Prince a gin and tonic. Casual attire is not encouraged. The two will always change for dinner; she into a short dress and the Duke into flannel trousers and a pullover. The only light comes from candles on the table.

The food, once more, will be simple. The Queen will have something like chicken casserole with creamy mushroom sauce, stuffed cabbage or poached haddock. They might have some wine but the Duke prefers beer (not so acid) and Perrier water.

The Queen seen at a State banquet in Canada in 1976.

Chicken, game or fish (always boned) may be on the menu but garlic is forbidden for obvious reasons. Cheese is not served at dinner but HM does enjoy chocolate mints when coffee, cognac and liqueurs are served.

Holiday time at Balmoral (usually from August to the beginning of October) is known as a "fattening break" for the Queen. She will indulge in baps and oatcakes while she and the rest of the royal family have regular picnics in the surrounding Highlands when venison pate, ham, chicken and plum pudding is eaten.

Prince Philip also enjoys barbecuing (he's said not to be as good a chef as he thinks he is!) and they all love eating al fresco.

At 5 o'clock, tea is served in the Queen's sitting room when a table is covered with a pretty lace-edged table cloth and there are two knives for each person. A steel bladed one for bread and butter and a silver bladed one for cakes. This is the most relaxing time of the day for the royals.

The Queen prefers Darjeeling tea and requires it to be brewed for three minutes. Prince Philip cleverly converted her Victorian silver spirit kettle to electricity. The Queen then pours milk from a silver jug, shaped like a cow, and will not allow one tea leaf to escape.

For a formal dinner which is always at 8pm the Queen will wear a long dress (with plenty of jewellery including a tiara) while the men invariably wear white tie and tails or, occasioanlly, black tie and dinner jackets.

The cutlery is laid out for the first and second courses after which the footmen will brush away the crumbs and add more cutlery for pudding or fruit which is known as dessert.

The dogs are not forgotten. A footman lays out a tablecloth on the floor and then brings in dishes of cooked meats, biscuits and gravy along with empty (silver) dog bowls. The Queen then mixes the dogs' food and, using a silver spoon and fork, places it in their bowls.

Prince Charles once commented:" In our family, everything stops for tea. I have never known a family so addicted to it."

The Queen herself says:" Such a cosy meal. We are not interested in alcohol."

Previous page
The Queen gives a speech at a State banquet held in St.George's Hall, Windsor Castle in 2000. The banquet was given in honour of President Herzog of Germany.

Above
A lavish banquet is given for the Queen during her visit to Kuala Lumpur, Malaysia in 1989.

Right
A typical tray setting for afternoon tea at Balmoral Castle. Dundee cake is often a favourite choice.

By Jennie Bond

Travelling around the world reporting on the Queen, it's easy to become quite blasé about the stunning array of jewellery that she wears. It might be a windy day in Warsaw or a scorcher in Sydney, but you can be sure that she will be immaculate in her pearls or diamonds and, in the evening, a tiara with all the trimmings.

The Queens' Jewels

Wherever she goes, a selection of priceless necklaces, earrings and brooches go with her, all carefully chosen to complement her outfits. Every item of jewellery she's been given on visits abroad is logged so that she can wear it on return trips. I have watched her at many a State Banquet dazzling the assembled company but, as far as the Queen is concerned, the jewellery is part of the uniform; she knows people expect to see royalty dripping with riches and she doesn't intend to disappoint them.

After fifty years as sovereign, the Queen's private collection has grown to fabulous proportions, largely due to the many gifts she's received on her travels. According to one estimate it's now worth more than £70 million. But it can't rival the universal symbol of the British Monarchy: the Crown Jewels, which she wears on great state occasions. A glittering display of coronation regalia, crowns and insignia dating back to the eleventh century, the jewels belong to the nation and are housed in the Tower of London where they attract more than two and a half million visitors a year.

The best known piece is the Imperial State Crown, worn by monarchs since Queen Victoria for the procession from Westminster Abbey after their coronation. It's also used at the State Opening of Parliament. The present crown is about the tenth version since the Restoration of Charles II and it's the same design as one made for Queen Victoria in

Left
The Queen wears a tiara made of huge aquamarines and diamonds. She had this tiara made to match the necklace and earrings that were a gift from the President and people of Brazil in 1953.

Inset
State Opening of Parliament, London in 1989. The Queen wears the Imperial State crown.

Above
Crown Jewels

Below
The Imperial State Crown carried in procession to the State Opening of Parliament.

1838. That one almost came to grief in 1845 when the Duke of Argyll dropped it during the opening of Parliament. Queen Victoria remarked that the crumpled crown looked "like a pudding that had sat down". It was re-made in 1937 for the coronation of George VI using practically the same stones and is set with 2,868 diamonds, 17 sapphires, 11 emeralds, 5 rubies and 273 pearls. The crown weighs a hefty 2lbs 13 ozs and is taken to Buckingham Palace each year before the Queen sets off for Parliament so that she can get used to its weight. At the front it boasts the Second Star of Africa, a 317.4-carat stone cut from the famous Cullinan diamond.

The Cullinan was discovered in 1905 by a mining superintendent in the Transvaal who thought it was a piece of shiny glass. When it was prised out of the wall it was found to be more than three inches long, weighing well over a pound. The miners decided it was too big to be worth anything so threw it out of a window. Luckily, the superintendent had his doubts. He retrieved it and, out of curiosity, had it analysed. The piece of "glass" turned out to be a diamond weighing 3,106 carats. The South African government announced they would give it to King Edward VII as a "token of the loyalty and attachment of the people of Transvaal." To ensure its safe passage to Britain, they pulled one of the neatest and most daring bluffs you could imagine. Police officers escorted what appeared to be the diamond on board a steamer, ceremoniously deposited it in the captain's safe and guarded it night and day until the boat arrived in London. Meanwhile the real diamond had been sent off by ordinary parcel post. It was presented to the King at a ceremony at Sandringham, his Norfolk home.

The largest cut from the diamond, known as the First Star of Africa, is set in the Sceptre with the Cross, an integral part of the Coronation ceremony. Seven more large diamonds from the Cullinan are now in royal brooches, a necklace and a ring.

Another important piece on display is the ancient St Edward's Crown, made for Charles II in 1662. The frame, monde and cross are all of gold, set with 440 precious or semi-precious stones. It weighs nearly five pounds, so it's fortunate that the Queen only had to wear it for the most sacred part of the coronation ceremony, the crowning itself.

Among the other treasures in the Tower is Queen Mary's Crown made by Garrard for the 1911 coronation. Its style is traditional, set in silver with over 2000 diamonds. The Crown worn by Queen Elizabeth the Queen Mother, and on display at her funeral, is the only one mounted in platinum and was created by Garrard for the Queen consort at the coronation in 1937. It has 2800 diamonds, the best known of which is the Koh-I-Noor (Mountain of Light). Until the Cullinan was discovered it was the largest known diamond in the world.

The remaining crowns in the royal collection include the Imperial Crown of India, specially created in 1911 for George V to be crowned King Emperor at the Delhi Durbar, two Prince of Wales's Crowns (one was made for Frederick Louis, son of George 11, in 1729, the other was worn by Edward VIII when he was Prince of Wales) and Queen Victoria's Small Diamond Crown. As its name suggests, this is the smallest in the collection standing only 3.7 inches high. Victoria wore it on top of her widow's cap.

Despite the extraordinary choice of jewellery that she can call on, the present Queen - following her mother - tends to wear the same pieces fairly frequently. Many have sentimental connections. They include 14 tiaras, 34 pairs of earrings, 98 brooches, 46 necklaces, 37 bracelets, 5 pendants, 14 watches and 15 rings. Her personal favourite is said to be the diamond engagement ring Prince Philip designed for her nearly 60 years ago. The diamonds came from a tiara that belonged to his mother and he had the ring made to his design by the London firm of Philip Antrobus. It is set with 11 diamonds, a central solitaire stone of 3 carats with five smaller stones in each shoulder. Unfortunately when Philip presented it to his future bride it turned out to be too big and had to be altered.

Above
The Queen wears the Grand Vladimir's tiara and earrings that later belonged to Queen Mary.

This Page
Top left - Diamond scrolls and festoon tiara. Worn Malaysia 1989.
2nd down - Diamond and pearl tiara worn in South Africa
3rd down - The Russian fringe tiara worn in Germany in 1992.
4th down - Queen Mary's festoon tiara worn with family orders and necklace to banquet in London in 1989.

Opposite Page
Diamond diadem – Queen Victoria's Jubilee necklace.

Though many people may not realise it, the piece of Crown Jewellery they see most often is the George IV State Diadem. It's the one the Queen wore in the procession to Westminster Abbey for her coronation. She wears it each year to and from Parliament. But the reason it's so well-known is because it's the crown the Queen wears on all postage stamps.

The single most valuable piece of jewellery owned by the Queen is a brooch she inherited from her grandmother, Queen Mary, who amassed a huge collection. It contains two of the Cullinan diamonds, known as the lesser Stars of Africa, if stones of 94.4 and 63.6 carats respectively can ever be known as lesser. The Queen refers to the brooch as "Granny's chips" and it's said to be worth £25 million.

Queen Mary also bequeathed three quite stunning tiaras to her granddaughter. One, of interlaced circles of diamonds, was originally made for the Grand Duchess Vladimir of Russia. Another Russian tiara, encrusted with 488 diamonds, was given to Princess Alexandra on her silver wedding in 1888. The third tiara with 19 pearl drops hanging below a lover's knot in diamonds was made for Queen Mary herself in 1914. Almost seventy years later, the Queen handed it on to the Princess of Wales as a wedding gift.

The jewels Elizabeth always calls "my best diamonds" were also her first. On her 21st birthday in 1947 she was in South Africa with her parents. The day was declared a public holiday and Government presented the Princess with a silver casket containing a long chain necklace of 21 large diamonds, the largest of which was 10 carats. She was standing near a microphone as it was handed to her by Field-Marshal Jan Smuts, and everyone heard her gasp of delight. Since then she's had the necklace shortened and a matching bracelet made.

On that same visit, she was given a platinum brooch set with 300 diamonds from the schoolchildren of what was then Southern Rhodesia. It was in the shape of the national flower, the flame lily. And it was that brooch that Elizabeth was wearing after the death of her father in 1952 when she flew back to London for the first time as Queen.

Perhaps the most personal pieces of jewellery the Queen has are the Royal Family Orders. More badge than brooch, they are miniature portraits of the monarch painted on ivory with a diamond border. A new Family Order is established at the start of each reign and is in the personal gift of the Sovereign. The Queen wears the Orders of her grandfather, King George V and her father George VI. They are worn with evening dress only or on State occasions, attached to silk ribbon on the left shoulder. The colour of the ribbon is chosen by each monarch; the Queen's is chartreuse yellow, her father's is rose pink.

For all her diamonds, emeralds and rubies if there is one gemstone forever associated with royalty it is the pearl. Queen Victoria started a family tradition by giving each of her five daughters two pearls a year from birth so that they would have necklaces when they grew up. George VI followed suit by presenting his baby daughter, Elizabeth with a thin platinum chain to which he added two pearls a year. To this day, the Queen is rarely seen out without a string of pearls - even at family barbecues.

As she celebrates her Golden Jubilee, the Queen is only too aware that the image of royalty is changing. But for the time being, the jewels remain very much part of the traditional image - and, as far as many schoolchildren are concerned, that's just as it should be. A memory I shall always treasure is of a four-year-old boy deep in Australia's outback. As the Queen walked into his classroom he looked up and, in a loud voice, demanded: "Where's your crown then?" She explained that it was locked up in a tower and she wasn't allowed to bring it with her. The boy was less than impressed by this lack of regal influence, and turned away to play with a dumper truck – leaving the Queen, her pearls and matching earrings, looking quietly amused. Time, perhaps, to roll out those diamonds.

THE QUEEN'S *Homes*

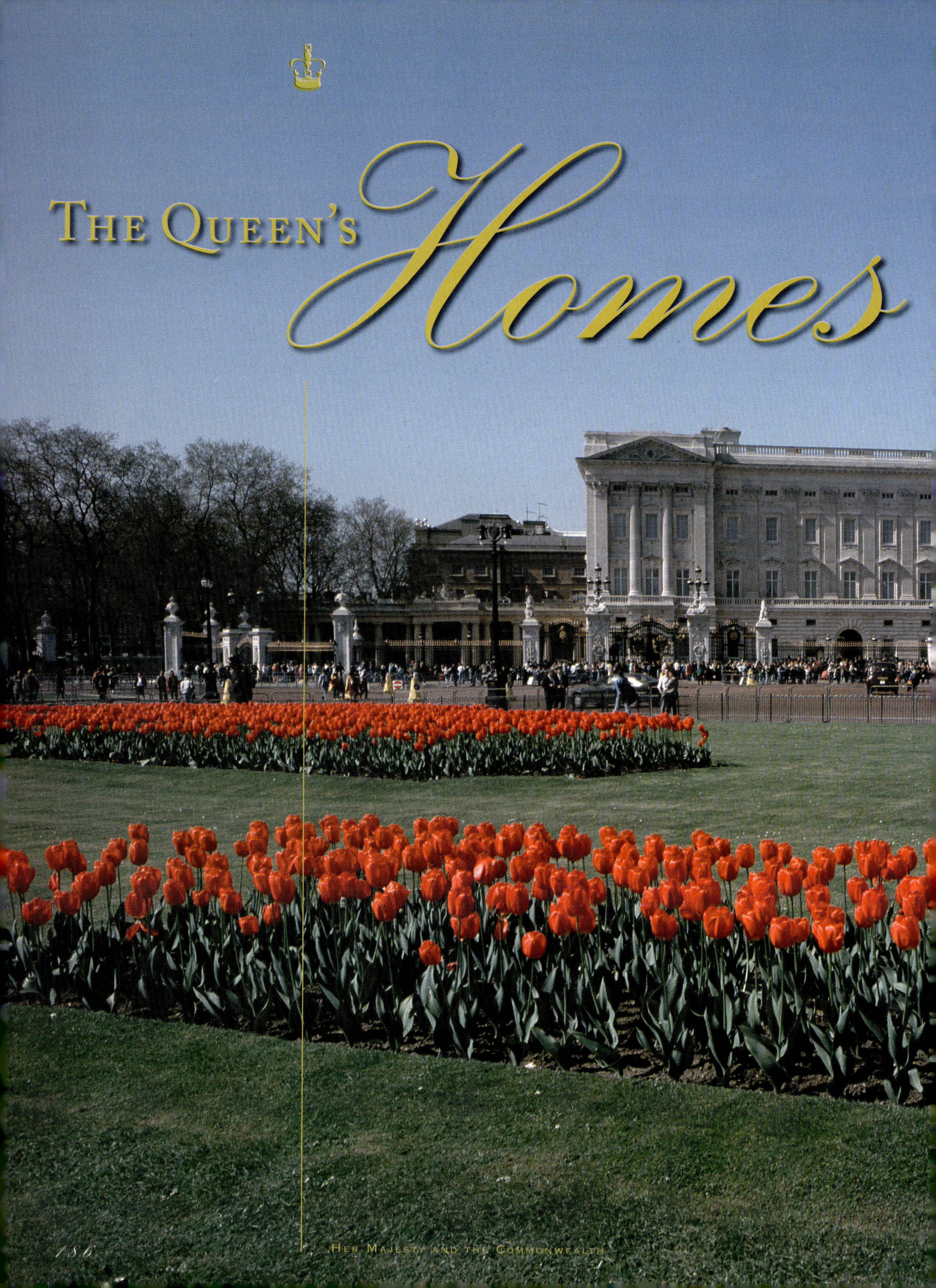

Previous page
Buckingham Palace, London in the Spring.

This Page
Guards march past Buckingham Palace, London towards the Queen Victoria Statue.

Above
Sandringham House on the Queen's Norfolk estate.

Right
The Palace of Holyrood nestling in the hills in Edingburgh, Scotland.

Above
Windsor Castle seen from the long walk.

Right
Balmoral Castle, Scotland. One of the Queen's favourite homes.

A Collection Most Regal

By Dickie Arbiter

Officially, and perhaps modestly, the Royal Collection is referred to as 'one' of the finest collections in the world. In reality it is probably 'the' finest, most diverse, largest and most valuable private collection anywhere.

With over a million individual items, it is practically impossible to pinpoint the best or greatest - after all beauty is in the eye of the beholder. To some it might be the collection of Michelangelo and Leonardo da Vinci drawings, undoubtedly the most valuable single collection. While to others it could well be the solitary picture of Vermeer's The Music Lesson in Buckingham Palace's Picture Gallery; or the bullet that killed Admiral Lord Nelson at Trafalgar on view in the Grand Vestibule at Windsor Castle. As for the most valuable - it's impossible to put a price tag on art work that is totally irreplaceable.

Amassed by successive sovereigns - since the reign of Charles I (1625-1649) - the collection was put together as interior decoration for the royal palaces and residences. It reflects the royal likes and dislikes, taste, and in some instances lack of it, friendships and love.

There are pictures by all the great masters, Canaletto, Rubens, Van Dyck, Rembrandt, Zoffany, Cuyp, Gainsborough, Reynolds, Lely, Holbein, Raphael, Titian and Vermeer. But somehow they failed to collect any Turners or Constables, although there are a few contemporary works by Cuneo and Sutherland tucked away. There's porcelain by Sèvres; English and French furniture dating from the 16th century, china, arms and armour, books, jewels. The list goes on endlessly.

So who were the great collectors? Some of the items dating back to Henry VIII (1509-1547) still survive, but it was Charles I who is largely credited with the formation of the collection. Sadly during the Interregnum (1649-1660) Oliver Cromwell got rid of the collection. Some of it was bought by the remnants of English nobility, to be returned to the sovereign at the Restoration of the Monarchy in 1660, while much of it was lost to foreign predators.

Credit, therefore, must go to the extravagant tastes of George IV (1820-1830) who collected anything and everything he could get his hands on. It really didn't matter how much it cost as long as he could have it.

He bought pictures, substantial quantities of silver gilt and English and French furniture. He built up a collection of French clocks and an unrivalled collection of Sèvres porcelain, all to furnish and decorate Carlton House. On the death of his father George III, and following the refurbishment of Buckingham House into a Palace in the 1820s, everything was moved out of Carlton House and into "his" Palace where much has of it has remained to this day.

Queen Victoria (1837-1901) had a good eye for art works, and together with Prince Albert, added to the collection through their patronage of artists such as Winterhalter, Frith and Landseer.

Portrait of King Charles I from three positions by Van Dyck.

Queen Anne, Georges I and II, William IV, Edward VII, and George V were not collectors in the real sense but in their own ways made a contribution.

For example, there's William IV's 'statue of guilt'. From 1790 the love affair between William, as Duke of Clarence, and Dora Jordan, one of the leading actresses of the day, was the talk of the country and the social set. The relationship lasted twenty years during which time she bore him ten children. But by the end of the first decade of the 19th century, William, already in mid-forties, was looking to his future and marriage, and neither included, the, by now, plump and motherly Dora. Following the break in the relationship, Dora's career went into decline and in 1816 she died sick, penniless and broken in Paris.

Two years after her death, William found his bride when he married Adelaide, a German princess. Whether he still carried a torch for Dora, or was ridden with guilt, is not known but when he became king in 1830 he commissioned Francis Chantrey to sculpt a statue of Dora, which he then intended having placed in Westminster Abbey. But the Dean of Westminster had other ideas. He told the king that under no circumstances would he allow the statue in the Abbey. So for the next hundred and twenty years the statue disappeared - until 1956 - when it appeared at a show at the Royal Academy.

It had another public outing, again at the Royal Academy in 1972 and in 1975 the Earl of Munster, one of Dora's descendants, gave the statue - Mrs Jordan and Two Children - to The Queen who had it placed in the Buckingham Palace Picture Gallery where it has been ever since.

Fabergé is a notable part of the Royal Collection. There are over five hundred pieces collected by each of the 20th century monarchs. Edward VII commissioned a series of Sandringham animals. George V purchased the Mosaic and Colonnade Imperial Easter eggs and George VI added cigarette cases.

Queen Mary's Dolls' House at Windsor, designed and built between 1921 and 1924, was donated to Queen Mary as a token of the nation's goodwill and gratitude to the King and the Queen for their duty to the nation during World War I. Designed by Sir Edwin Lutyens, who was still busy at the time building New Delhi, the house was a model of an English gentleman's house of the early 1920s.

It has over forty rooms and lifts that stop at every floor. There is electric light, hot and cold running water in all of the five bathrooms and lavatories that flush. Built on a scale of 1: 12 inches (2.5cms: 30.5cms) the house is 102 inches (2.6m) long and 60 inches (1.52m) high. Lutyens coordinated the ideas of nearly fifteen hundred tradesmen, artists and authors.

The paintings are real as are the books; in fact everything about the Dolls' House is real and a testimony to British craftsmanship of the day. It was the centrepiece of the British Empire Exhibition in 1924 after which Queen Mary said it should always be on show and that proceeds from the sale of tickets should fund some of the Queen's charitable schemes, a practise that continues to this day. The Dolls' House has been at Windsor since 1925

Statue of 'Mrs Jordan' by Sir Francis Chantrey.

It was also Queen Mary who transformed the Picture Gallery at Buckingham Palace. Big enough to accommodate two tennis courts, it was designed to be a showcase for art but was something of a failure. The roof leaked, there wasn't enough light to see the pictures and Queen Victoria had practically every inch of wall space covered in exhibits.

It remained in its cluttered form, with leaking roof, right through the reign of Edward VII until 1914 when at Queen Mary's suggestion a glazed arched ceiling was installed, the door cases simplified and a vast number of pictures removed to be hung elsewhere.

Not strictly part of the Royal Collection of art but a royal collection nevertheless, the Royal Philatelic Collection is probably the world's largest collection of British and Commonwealth stamps. Since the Penny Black of 1840 every definitive issue of stamp has carried the portrait of the monarch. Stamps have been a major source of pleasure to monarchs, particularly George V. His interest in stamps began as a childhood hobby and developed into a passion. He was so knowledgeable that the Royal Philatelic Society elected him Honorary Vice President when he was only 28.

Three years later he became executive President, and Patron on becoming king in 1910. As Duke of York he paid, in 1904, £1,450 for a single stamp - about £60,000 in today's money. One Royal anecdote has it that following the auction a courtier greeted him with the words - "did Your Royal Highness hear that some damned fool has just paid £1,450 for a single stamp?" "I was that damned fool", the future Monarch is said to have replied.

Colonnade Egg clock by Carl Faberge.

On behalf of the Directors and staff of The Royal Bank of Scotland Group I am pleased to extend our warmest wishes to Her Majesty The Queen on the occasion of her Golden Jubilee.

Sir George Mathewson
Chairman

MAID'S ROOM
KING'S WARDROBE
KING'S BEDROOM

Throughout his reign he spent at least three afternoons a week on his beloved stamps and by the time of the his death in 1936 the collection had grown to fill 325 red stamp albums each containing about 50 pages. The exact number of individual stamps is not known but runs into tens if not hundreds of thousands. The collection has grown considerably in The Queen's 50-year reign, and in addition to the albums there are some 200 boxes full of stamps kept at St James's Palace.

Perhaps one of the quirkiest pieces of art history in the Collection surrounds a portrait of Charles II. There is nothing special about the portrait except where it comes from.

At the Restoration of the Monarchy in 1660 Charles II set about reinstating the old glories of the crown. Windsor Castle had suffered under Cromwell, and the king, through his architect Hugh May, commissioned the Italian artist Antonio Verio to produce painted decorations in the Castle apartments. Much of Verio's work can still be seen today but what is lost forever are his paintings in St George's Hall depicting the history of Edward III and the Black Prince and the Order of the Garter.

When George IV became king in 1820 he redesigned the Castle's apartments and instructed his architect Jeffry Wyatville that his new designs should include nothing of Charles II's St George's Hall. Wyatville carried out the king's instructions and completely destroyed the Verio ceiling - or so he said. In 1997 the Charles II portrait, originally painted into Verio's ceiling, mysteriously turned up at a saleroom in Vienna.

No one knows how it got there or where it had come from, but it was authenticated and bought by a London art dealer and subsequently purchased by The Queen. It had disappeared for 150 years but is now back at Windsor hanging in the upper gallery of the Lantern Lobby, near to where it was all those years ago.

The Royal Collection is managed by the Royal Collection Trust and is probably the only major collection in the United Kingdom that receives no financial donations or public funding. Through opening the Palace and Windsor Castle doors to the public it has become totally self-financing.

The Queen will not go down in the history as one of the great Royal collectors. But as sovereign and custodian she has ensured that this valuable private collection, which she does not own personally, remains in tact. Arguably she has done more than any of her predecessors to make the collection accessible to the wider general public through the opening of Buckingham Palace, more access to Windsor Castle and the Palace of Holyroodhouse. Two galleries have been built in her name, in London and Edinburgh and she has ensured there are frequent loans to exhibitions at home and abroad.

Few of the monarchs down the ages, even the acquisitive George IV, can be credited with a great artistic vision. Yet the Royal Collection is an engaging reflection of the eclectic, often eccentric tastes of this idiosyncratic group of wealthy individuals we are proud to call our Monarchy.

View of the Queen Mary's dolls house.

100 Facts About Her Majesty

By James Whitaker

The Queen has lived in the full glare of publicity, often unhappily. Holidays spent at Balmoral or Sandringham provide much needed relief from the incessant media attention. Whilst there, she expects total loyalty from her friends, family and staff to protect her privacy. And in the main they oblige. But during the past 76 years, snippets of "what she's really like" have crept out, revealing her tastes, her habits, her sense of humour, even her quirks. Some might say her "ordinariness".

Here are 100 examples of what makes this remarkable woman tick.

1 At the tender age of 11 she went on the Civil List and was granted £6,000 a year. It is now £7,900,000.

2 The Queen has a favourite tiara that can be taken apart and used as a necklace, two clips and a bracelet.

3 Adolf Hitler described the then Princess Elizabeth as "Ein fabelhaftes kind" (a marvellous child).

4 The Queen does not like cats.

5 She enjoys jigsaw puzzles.

6 Everywhere she travels, Malvern water (still) goes with her. Another favourite tipple is Mateus Rosé.

7 Not only does the Queen own racehorses, but racing pigeons too. Their bloodline comes from birds owned by her great grandfather Edward V11. They're kept in Norfolk.

8 In 1945, she was thrown from her horse, bruising both legs.

9 As a child she nicknamed her music teacher, Mabel Lauder, "Goosey".

10 Two Chinese Chow dogs - Blackie and Brownie - would guard her as a one-year-old.

11 The first time she ever set foot in hospital, as a patient, was in 1982 - with toothache.

12 It was not until she was a 4-year-old that HM first saw the sea – at Bognor. She was said to be not impressed.

13 If so ordered by Prime Minister Tony Blair, she would have to sign her own death warrant.

14 The Queen insisted that Prince Charles, like everybody else in 1948, should have a green ration card.

15 As well as sending out birthday telegrams to 100 year olds, she sends messages to those celebrating their Diamond (60th) wedding and, thereafter, for 65th, 70th and every following anniversary.

16 The Queen is 5'4" and has size 5 feet.

17 The Queen was taught tennis by the coach at Eton but now finds it boring.

18 She was rebuffed by Sir Winston Churchill when he refused a Dukedom "or anything like that."

19 The Queen now voluntarily pays tax on her private income but sovereigns do not pay death duties.

20 In 1959, HM altered the Trooping the Colour ceremony from Thursday to Saturday to lessen traffic congestion.

21 Her Will will never be revealed.

22 All her life, HM has kept a personal diary which has never been seen by anybody else.

23 Her favourite game has always been charades which is played each Christmas.

24 HM never wears a hard hat while riding or seat belts while driving around her estates.

25 While travelling abroad, both privately and on official tours, her luggage is sealed in tamper proof containers that not even customs officials may inspect.

26 All her shoes come from Rayne.

27 A solid silver mascot of St George and the dragon is transferred to whichever official car she is using.

28 She was once the leader of the Woodpecker Patrol of the Buckingham Palace Girl Guides.

29 She is the 42nd monarch since William the Conqueror.

30 Prince Philip's nickname for the Queen is "sausage".

31 Her favourite film is Yellow Submarine.

32 Queen Elizabeth 11 was the first sovereign to be proclaimed Head of the Commonwealth.

33 The Queen was aged seven when she first looked after a corgi called Dookie which belonged to her father.

34 Of all the members of the royal family she is the only one not allowed to vote.

35 As a baby she did not crawl as other children. She sat almost upright on one leg and "sculled" with the other.

36 She cannot be sued in court - or give evidence.

37 Her milk bottles have the royal cipher (EIIR). It is said that first seeing these ciphers convinced her she was the Queen.

38 The Queen takes snake venom to prevent varicose veins and poison ivy to counter the arthritis from which both she and Prince Philip suffer.

39 As a child she received one shilling (5p) a week, later increased to five shillings a week.

40 Each Maundy Thursday (just before Easter) the Queen distributes specially minted coins to twice as many people as her age.

41 The central jewel on the Queen's crown, the Koh-i-Noor, brings bad luck to any man and good luck to any woman who wears it.

42 To boost her energy, the Queen sucks on barley sugar sweets.

43 She was the first monarch to accede to a throne while up a tree – in Kenya.

44 As a toddler, she owned a chair that played music when she sat on it.

45 The Queen if she chose, could make everyone a peer and declare war.

46 HM has three inalienable rights with regard to her Ministers. To be consulted, to warn and to encourage.

47 While at work in her study at Buckingham Palace she kicks off her shoes.

48 The Prime Minister and Cabinet are her servants, dependent on her consent to give authority to their every action. They can only "advise" her, never "command" only recommend.

49 You call her Ma'am (rhyming with jam, not charm). Your Majesty is for documents and formal occasions.

50 Officially, HM has no opinions and for that reason she never gives interviews.

51 The predecessors she admires most are her grand-parents, King George V and Queen Mary. Before them, her greatest idol, her great-great-grandmother Queen Victoria.

52 The Queen regards her Christmas Day broadcast as one of her most important responsibilities.

53 On one tour, a photographer dropped his glass of whisky at her feet while talking to HM at a reception and, later, his flash gun failed to go off. "Just not your day" she commented sympathetically.

54 As a teenager she shot a stag but, nowadays, she does not shoot at all. Instead, she hosts the lunches for the "guns" and picks up birds.

55 The Queen speaks good French.

56 It is said that her favourite Head of State of all time is Nelson Mandela.

57 HM refuses to let her friends or staff reveal her favourite Christmas hymn. She's concerned that if the name got out, it would be sung constantly.

58 When Britain wins a battle, commented Churchill, she shouts "God save the Queen." When she loses, she votes down the prime minister.

59 When handing out gifts she gives Shetland scarves or wooden boxes made by Lord Linley, the son of Princess Margaret.

60 When she's tired of talking to you, she takes a backward step and smiles broadly.

61 On tour, she avoids garlic, shellfish and spaghetti for obvious reasons.

62 HM enjoys crosswords, particularly the more difficult one in the Daily Telegraph.

63 On her wedding day (November 20 1947) there was a bunch of white carnations on her breakfast tray, a gift from Prince Philip.

64 As a child, her favourite poem was They're Changing Guard at Buckingham Palace.

65 Thanks to television, Elizabeth 11 was the first British Sovereign truly to be crowned as the rubric requires "in the sight of all the people."

66 The only "Classic" race not won by the Queen is the Derby. Aureole went very close in Coronation Year, 1953.

67 Wherever she goes, the Queen takes a black dress - and black-lined notepaper - in the event of the need for instant mourning.

68 The Queen is said to have sworn only once. The early morning when Michael Fagan broke into her Palace bedroom and sat on her bed. When a policeman eventually appeared she said "Get a bloody move on."

69 Her favourite servant of all time was her maid, Bobo MacDonald who slept in the same bedroom as Elizabeth as a child. Bobo who had more access to HM than any other "outsider" died in 1993.

70 The reason that the Queen will never abdicate is because she took a Holy vow while being anointed with oil, no to so do. She's a deeply Christian woman.

71 Her regular travelling companions include a feather pillow, a monogrammed electric kettle and a white kid lavatory seat.

72 When asked what he talked about with the Queen at their weekly meetings, Churchill would reply "Racing."

73 The Queen does not have a passport or a number plate on her official cars.

74 She will not have 13 sit down at the same table. If this looks a possibility, she divides her guests into two tables.

75 Her advice to those about to stand for a long time is "Place your weight evenly between your two legs and sway gently."

76 She keeps little in her handbag. Reading glasses, a perfumed handkerchief and keys to open the dispatch boxes that contain her state papers.

77 When Norman Hartnell made her white satin Coronation dress he secretly embroidered a four-leaf shamrock into the skirt "for luck". This was only discovered in 1993 when the dress was loaned for an exhibition.

78 While searching for ducks' eggs at the lake in the gardens of Buckingham Palace, she fell in as a child.

79 The Queen used to hunt. The first time was when, as a 5 year old, she rode to hounds with the Pytchley.

80 The very first word she spoke was "mummy". She called King George VI "Papa".

81 The first time she appeared on the cover of Time magazine was when she was aged 3 for "setting a major fashion trend" by wearing a yellow dress.

82 When the King and Queen toured Australia and New Zealand at the end of the Twenties, they were given toys for the then Princess Elizabeth weighing three tons.

83 Although agreeing to the famous 60's television film Royal Family, the Queen was okay with the camera lenses but unhappy with the microphones. She said:" I'll sound so silly and trite."

84 HM has always said that if her time is ever up, and she's no longer wanted as Head of State, that she will "go quietly."

85 The Queen does not live informally, even at her country house, Sandringham. There are plenty of footmen on duty, properly liveried with brass buttons and red waistcoats.

86 Dinner is served at 8.30 p.m. promptly and the Queen will have organised for her guests to have had their clothes unpacked for them and then pressed before being placed on wooden hangers all burnt with EIIR by pokers.

87 The Queen spends hours looking at the stars and knows most of the constellations.

88 HM is one of the most knowledgeable people in the country on racehorse blood lines.

89 After years of dying her hair with a rinse called "chocolate kiss" she stopped doing so in 1990.

90 The Queen's blood group is O-negative.

91 Comments sent each day on her web site are printed out and given to her.

92 Like her grandmother, Queen Mary, the Queen hates ivy.

93 In 1941 she was Principal Boy, playing Prince Florizel, in a Windsor Castle wartime pantomime.

94 Her first ever piece of personal jewellery was, at nine months, a string of pink coral beads from the Queen Mother. The necklace was passed on to Princess Anne at the same age.

95 To keep her conversations secret, a "scrambler" is fitted to her telephone.

96 Although she uses a computer more and more, she still writes in ink. Her blotting paper is black to keep her writings private and is destroyed at the end of each day.

97 On her 16th birthday, she registered at the Windsor Labour Exchange.

98 When telephone operators connected the Queen to the Queen Mother each morning, they would say:" Your Majesty? Her Majesty, Your Majesty."

99 When the Queen is angry she drums her fingers.

100 When she's REALLY angry with somebody she says "How amusing" and then walks away.